DATE DUE

DE 19 '08			

DEMCO 38-296

THE AMERICAN APPROACH TO FOREIGN AFFAIRS

An Uncertain Tradition

ROGER S. WHITCOMB

Westport, Connecticut
London

Library of Congress Cataloging-in-Publication Data

Whitcomb, Roger S., 1939–
    The American approach to foreign affairs : an uncertain tradition
 / Roger S. Whitcomb.
      p. cm.
    Includes bibliographical references and index.
    ISBN 0–275–96099–4 (alk. paper)
    1. United States—Foreign relations—Philosophy. I. Title.
 E183.7.W64   1998
  327.73—dc21   97–35139

British Library Cataloguing in Publication Data is available.

Library of Congress Catalog Card Number: 97–35139
ISBN: 0–275–96099–4

First published in 1998

Praeger Publishers, 88 Post Road West, Westport, CT 06881
An imprint of Greenwood Publishing Group, Inc.

Printed in the United States of America

∞™

The paper used in this book complies with the
Permanent Paper Standard issued by the National
Information Standards Organization (Z39.48–1984).

10 9 8 7 6 5 4 3 2

For Roberta, whose boundless faith and
encouragement
can only be acknowledged,
never fully repaid.

Contents

Preface: An American Paradox

This book represents an extensive inquiry into the historical panorama of America's tradition of foreign affairs. That tradition, out of which American foreign policy sprang and was nourished, yields up a number of admirable ideals: the preservation and enhancement of human dignity, freedom, equality, justice, well-being, peace, order, and stability. But their strengths as reflections of America's national morality are at the same time their weakness as descriptions for programs of external action. They convey great and serious meaning to human beings most everywhere, but they have been insufficient throughout our history as vital ends of policy or as touchstones for selecting among available alternative means of action.

It is the author's intention in the six chapters that constitute this work to isolate, clarify, and critically evaluate the major components of that tradition as they unfolded over time. It should be noted at the outset that this book is not intended in any sense to be a comprehensive review of American foreign policy. Rather, it should be seen as an attempt to elucidate one important variable—that of America's tradition of foreign affairs—and to put that factor into some sort of proper historical perspective. The emphasis here is not so much one of examining in minute detail the historical contexts in which the various elements of this tradition were elaborated but, rather, of explicating and synthesizing those elements of that tradition that have conditioned the country's approach to the outside world during the first two centuries of its foreign relations and that still have applicability today.

It is in this sense that this book is concerned first and foremost with the "hidden side" of American foreign policy—those deep-seated influences, drawn from historical experience, that our public officials and the attentive publics who interact with them have tended to manifest in their dealings with others. It is a study of the psychological and social undercurrents—the mood, tone and climate of thought—that have constituted the framework for the generation of specific actions by our policy-makers. One conclusion that must be drawn from this study is most sobering indeed: There may well be more to be feared from America's approach to problems than the substance of the problems themselves.

It is both timely and appropriate in the wake of the end of the Cold War that a renewed effort be made to grasp the full meanings of that rich lode of tradition that has long generated the perceptual framework of America's world view. As the lone superpower in a world of inexorable transformation, America remains in a highly advantageous position to influence events for the foreseeable future. What it does will likely continue to represent a major variable in the fabric of international relations. A proper understanding of the mindset that constitutes the framework for its policymaking is therefore mandatory.

It is well to note in this regard that while there exists a rich and detailed literature dealing with most aspects of America's tradition of foreign affairs, there has been surprisingly little effort at broad-based synthesis. Whatever the reasons for this relative paucity, an understanding of the interrelated influences that have shaped America's world view is now more necessary than ever, as America engages in the process of helping to lay down the framework of a new post–Cold War international order.

It has been said that history is an argument without end and that it is the duty of historians to rewrite it constantly. If that be true, the record of the American foreign affairs experience would seem to lend itself well to this hard truth. If the ultimate issue before the American people concerns their prospects as a nation for dealing with the challenge of how to influence the contemporary tides of history with an effective design of their own, then by proclaiming broad goals but pursuing policies at odds with both its own most cherished values and the realities of international life, America will remain unfulfilled as a creative world force. More than that, it will continue to mislead itself into believing that because platitudes cannot easily be made into reality, the American people are limited to improvisation and sporadic counterpunching in their long-range planning and action. If we are to recover our perspective as a people and to merit "the decent respect of mankind," the American people must not only engage in serious self-examination but also generate fundamental change in their conduct. This book is aimed at making a contribution to this necessary act of national reconstruction.

Introduction: The American Tradition of Foreign Affairs

There is nothing more traditional, more molded by the history of the past, than the diplomacy of the nation-state, its perception of the world of international politics, and its conception of its role in that world. While nation-states are not necessarily captives of their histories, previous experiences (both successes and failures) form a context within which contemporary decision-makers evaluate alternatives.

National traditions are reflections of basic values (*grundnorms*) that have characterized the conduct of successive generations of inhabitants of particular countries. These traditions are verbal symbols that express ideas and ideals venerated in the histories of these countries.[1] They also consist of marked traits that may be seen to epitomize the behavior of a given country—at the very least reflective of the state's habitual conduct—in its relationships with others. Those traits, taken together, represent the habit of action and decision that derives from the assumptions that are made about political reality. We may call these traits the national style. If politics is a living art in which specific conditions and distinctions make some difference, style in great measure influences the choices that have to be made.

National traditions, then, *are the values and traits that may be said to inform and characterize the behavior of a state's population over time.* While members of particular countries certainly differ in their individualities, their common denominator values and traits comprise a basic "personality structure," formed as they mature within their cultural environments. Being embedded so firmly in popular political consciousness, these traditions represent relatively constant and fixed factors that must be taken into account by those who would develop a well-grounded understanding of the substance of any country's contemporary foreign policy. These traditions have significance, not so much because they are or are not objective responses to reality but because they strongly influence what we do in the here and now.

THE METHODOLOGICAL PROBLEM

The employment of tradition as a conceptual framework for analyzing a state's foreign policy is not without its difficulties.[2] These conceptual problems must be dealt with if the notion of tradition is to be utilized with any meaning and validity. For one thing, speaking of an entire nation-state in terms of so-called characteristic values and behavior traits entails some rather large-scale generalizing, with all of the attendant dangers that such assertions imply. To be sure, these generalizations tend to lose specificity as descriptions of any "real" people or even when dealing with particular issues. An important question is whether or ot each ation possesses an actual topology or range of traditions different from other nations. Do traditions vary from nation to nation? There is no simple answer to that question.

Then, too, one can become a hostage to one's own prior assumptions, erroneously assigning to a national people a collective personality, ascribing to it mythical common traditions. In this sense, the employment of tradition may well be a vehicle for the verbalization of the observer's own biases and idiosyncrasies. And yet, no matter what the observer's own prejudices, the point remains: If *no* distinctive national traditions in fact exist, then neither can there be a nationalism; if there is no such thing as a national character, then there are no real clear-cut distinctions that differentiate nations. For any analyst sensitive to the realities of history, it is difficult to accept that conclusion.

Nevertheless, in order to subscribe to the notion of distinctive national traditions, two alternative explanations for the presence of such national exclusiveness must be confronted. First, a particular nation's traditions may in fact be reflective of more general human attributes and, therefore, not restricted merely to itself. Thus, for example, it may well be that the "moralism" and "utopianism" of which so many have noted (with approval or dismay) in America's historical conduct are not uniquely American traditions at all but human features expressive of many cultures, although, to be sure, manifested more strongly in some societies than in others. A second explanation suggests that the idea of national tradition is more a function of subjective assertions of friends and enemies. We tend, it is argued, to ascribe "good" values to our friends and "bad" values to our enemies. Undoubtedly, some evidence exists for this sort of behavior.[3] Certain traditions, doubtless, are common to all cultures, and the degree of amity and hostility among nations does impact the manner in which they view one another. With this caveat in mind, it nevertheless is still not inappropriate to posit that traditions also flourish in peculiarly national frameworks, unique to specific cultures and not contingent simply upon subjective perceptions of friends and enemies.

One difficulty here is that no precise or definitive list of such traditions has yet been delineated, either for America or for other countries. Those, for example, who have explored the subject of American traditions have not even agreed on a catalog of them.[4] And there is even less consensus among scholars as to the relative importance to give to the various ingredients of the American tradition that have been identified. But these circumstances, unsettling as they may be, do not demean tradition as an analytical concept or tool for those who seek insights in this area; rather, it is a commentary on the lack of research that social science has heretofore devoted to the subject.

Another problem inherent in the utilization of tradition as an analytical tool relates to the fact that national traditions can and do change. The fast-moving world of today has significantly impacted some of the historic traditions of the American people.[5] A country's conduct will be conditioned by stressful experiences, such as defeat in war, economic depression, or revolution. Moreover, human migration patterns—whether they be external immigration or internal urbanization—have an impact on the values held and approaches to problem-solving exhibited by states; so, too, do changes in the educational levels of populations. Tradition, therefore, should be regarded as a relative rather than an absolute quality, evolving gradually in response to changing conditions.

While tradition refers to relatively enduring personality characteristics and patterns that are modal among the adult members of society, it is also something that manifests itself as a tendency in the majority of members of a national group rather than as a universal attribute present in all of them. Tradition, moreover, changes only slowly, any given policy in the present being in large measure a reflection of past practice as it has undergone modifications over time. It is incumbent, then, upon the policy analyst to come to grips with this evolving reality—the marriage of the past to the present—and to build bridges of understanding for the policy-maker to reflect upon.

In the absence, therefore, of well-tested data, or even of widely accepted agreement, the commentary that follows is designed to help elucidate the void between image and reality in American foreign policy by reference to the role that tradition has played in America's perceptions of the world. To speak of "America" in somewhat sweeping terms, we shall be looking at the activities of those Americans who are responsible for and actively involved in the nation's foreign relations. To the degree that decision-makers and "the people" are bound together by a common impulse to action, they may be said to reflect that tradition in one fashion or another. An appreciation of America's traditions of foreign affairs is so vital to an adequate comprehension of its policies toward the outside world that it is better to make the effort, despite the dangers, in the hope of improving comprehension of the roots of that tradition and of the conflicts that it has helped to engender.[6]

THE FRAMEWORK OF TRADITION

America's traditions fall into three broad categories: first, environmental inducements—products of America's particular location in time and in space; second, abstract dogmas and moral imperatives—deeply felt and widely shared—that have determined the nation's goals and defined its conduct; and third, assumptions about human behavior that have served to generate methods of action designed to operationalize these elaborated goals.

The colonial era of America's historical development represented the incubation period during which many of these traditions first appeared and were internalized in the collective psyche of its people. America emerged from its colonial history possessed of certain ideas, guided by a range of ideals that, taken together, may be said to have comprised a sort of world view. That *Weltanschauung* has been derived from several elements: a marked geographical separation from the Old World, a rather salutary legacy of abundance, a provocative mix of indigenous cultural diversity and parochialism, the dynamics of its so-called Puritan heritage, a rather righteous self-image of uniqueness, a remarkable record of environmental transformation, and an uncommon sense of what might be labeled isolation in time. What has resulted from a continuing interaction of these factors is a pronounced distinctiveness in its foreign policy when compared to any other country on earth.

In terms of style, Americans have exhibited a number of traits that represent pivotal elements of the nation's mode of action in foreign affairs. These traits constitute a set of important patterns of action in the world as filtered through the prism of America's national experience. They are, first, a distinctive conceptualization of the world of action; second, a propensity to universalize its dominant values; third, a preference for legalisms in its dealings with others; and fourth, a crusading nationalist ideology.

In Chapters 1 and 2, we shall be examining the dominant values and traits that have historically characterized the conduct of those who have been responsible for, and actively involved in, America's foreign relations. In Chapter 3, we shall take a look at the policy imperatives and approaches to problem-solving exhibited by Americans as a consequence of these elaborated traditions. Chapter 4 engages in an in-depth examination of the country's historic isolationist-interventionist tendencies, with a special emphasis on the "spiritual" relationship between the two. In Chapter 5 the author critically examines America's alliance policy after the Second World War as a case study of the country's tradition of foreign affairs in action. Finally, Chapter 6 is both a brief summary recapitulation of the initial four chapters as well as an effort to put into clearer perspective the dilemma for twentieth-century American foreign policy that these traditions have come to entail.

Tocqueville thought democracies would do poorly in foreign affairs because "foreign politics demand scarcely any of those qualities which are peculiar to a democracy; they require, on the contrary, the perfect use of almost all those in which it is deficient."[7] The record of America in the world of the twentieth century bears disconcerting testimony to the veracity of the French sage's observations.

NOTES

1. Democracies, of course, are particularly dependent upon such symbols to make complex facts of international politics simple enough for the general public to grasp. See, in this regard, the classic study by Murray Edelman, *The Symbolic Uses of Politics* (Urbana: University of Illinois Press, 1967). See also Walter Lippmann, *The Public Philosophy* (Boston: Little, Brown, 1955).

2. The relationship of values and attitudes to political behavior is a complicated matter. Obviously, behavior is a function of both attitudes and environmental stimuli. A major challenge is to separate the common or aggregate behavioral traits from the idiosyncratic. Some analysts judge this task to be impossible on the basis that behavioral traits on a national level actually do not exist. See, for example, Henry Hamilton Fyfe, *The Illusion of National Character* (London: Watts and Co., 1940); and Maurice L. Farber, "The Problem of National Character: A Methodological Analysis," *Journal of Psychology* 30 (1950), pp. 307–316.

3. The precipitous transformation in the American perception of the Russian national character between 1944, when America and Soviet Russia were allies fighting a common enemy, and 1948, following the coup d'état in Czechoslovakia and the Russian blockade of Berlin, is a case in point. See, in this regard, William Welch, *American Images of Soviet Foreign Policy* (New Haven, Conn.: Yale University Press, 1970). For an excellent introduction to the question of the impact of belief systems on international affairs, see Ole R. Holsti, "The Belief System and National Images: A Case Study," *Journal of Conflict Resolution* 6, No. 3 (September, 1962), pp. 245–271. An important and relevant article on long-term opinion changes is that by Karl W. Deutsch and Richard L. Merritt, "Effects of Events on National and International Images," in Herbert Kelman, ed., *International Behavior: A Social-Psychological Analysis* (New York: Holt, Rinehart and Winston, 1965).

4. The literature on the American tradition as it relates to foreign policy is voluminous. What follows is a listing of what in this writer's view are some of the more insightful and provocative treatments: Luigi Giorgio Barzini, *Americans Are Alone in the World* (Freeport, N.Y.: Library Press, 1972); Denis W. Brogan, *The American Character*, rev. ed. (New York: W. W. Norton, 1944); Arthur A. Ekirch, Jr., *Ideas, Ideals and American Diplomacy* (New York: Appleton-Century-Crofts, 1966); Geoffrey Gorer, *The American People: A Study in National Character*, rev. ed. (New York: W.W. Norton, 1964); Norman A. Graebner, *Ideas and Diplomacy: Readings in the Intellectual Tradition of American Foreign Policy* (New York: Oxford University Press, 1964); Charles O. Lerche, Jr., and Abdul A. Said, *Foreign Policy of the American People*, 4th ed. (Englewood Cliffs, N.J.: Prentice-Hall, 1991); Margaret Mead, *And Keep Your Powder Dry: An Anthropologist Looks at America* (New York: William Morrow, 1942); David Riesman, *The Lonely Crowd* (New Haven, Conn.: Yale University Press, 1950); Frank Tannenbaum, *The American Tradition in Foreign Policy* (Norman, Okla.: University of Oklahoma Press, 1955); Cecil V. Crabb, Jr., *The Doctrines of American Foreign Policy: Their Meaning, Role, and*

Future (Baton Rouge: Louisiana State University Press, 1982). See also Lee Coleman, "What is American? A Study of Alleged American Traits," *Social Forces* 19 (May, 1941), pp. 492–499.

Examples of a more introspective literature on this subject written primarily by historians include: John M. Blum, *The Promise of America: An Historical Inquiry* (Boston: Houghton Mifflin, 1966); Daniel J. Boorstin, *The Americans: The National Experience* (New York: Random House, 1965); Henry Steele Commager, *The American Mind: An Interpretation of American Thought and Character since the 1880s* (New Haven, Conn.: Yale University Press, 1950); Ralph Henry Gabriel, *The Course of American Democratic Thought since 1815* (New York: Ronald Press Co., 1940); Hans Kohn, *American Nationalism: An Interpretative Essay* (New York: Macmillan, 1957); Max Lerner, *America as a Civilization* (New York: Simon & Schuster, 1957); Seymour Martin Lipset, *The First New Nation: The United States in Historical and Comparative Perspective* (New York: Basic Books, 1963); and Robert E. Spiller and Eric Larabee, eds., *American Perspective: The National Self-Image in the Twentieth Century* (Cambridge, Mass.: Harvard University Press, 1961).

5.   The isolationist tradition, for example, while still psychologically appealing for many Americans, has undergone important modifications as a result of the Second World War and the post-1945 Russian-American Cold War confrontation.

6.   Graham Allison and Robert Jervis, among others, have sought to bring the process of foreign policy analysis to a higher level of sophistication. See, for example, Allison's *Essence of Decision: Explaining the Cuban Missile Crisis* (Boston: Little, Brown, 1971); and Jervis', *Perception and Misperception in International Politics* (Princeton, N.J.: Princeton University Press, 1976).

7.   Alexis de Tocqueville's *Democracy in America* has undergone a number of translations into English since it was initially published. The one that will be utilized in these pages is the Vintage edition, edited by Phillips Bradley (New York: Vintage Books, 1958), Vols. 1–2; in this instance, 1, p. 243.

CHAPTER 1

Ideas, Ideals, and Ideology in American History

We are the most perfect society now existing in the world.
—Hector St. John Crèvecoeur

America owes its being as a separate society and national entity not simply to long-standing ethnic similarities or common historical traditions, as do many other nations, but to a series of conscious and deliberate commitments by many generations of its immigrants. From the first "pilgrims" down to the present day, successive waves of newcomers have sought to create and become part of a new society based on novel principles of social, economic, and political organization. In so doing, most of these peoples, in one fashion or another, have subscribed to what might be called an American national credo or purpose.

That purpose, from the Charter of James I to the contemporary women's and gay rights movements, has been the achievement of equality in freedom. In the American context, equality and freedom have possessed at least two attributes that have in essence determined the nature of our society and have, therefore, had a crucial impact upon its historic development. First, equality and freedom are idealistic conceptualizations that obtain their actual meaning from the substantive context with which they are imbued. As a society founded upon these concepts, America has been required to answer the questions: Equal with regard to what? Free from what? Equal and free for what? Characteristically, America, as epitomized in the writings of its most representative intellectuals, has not generated a single response to these questions but rather has elaborated a multiplicity of them. The diversity of these substantive responses derives from the various conceptions of an objective order that its people have endeavored to realize. That is the source of American pluralism in its domestic affairs. It is also the wellspring from which a number of major problems have arisen in the country's foreign affairs.

The second distinguishing feature of the American purpose of equality in freedom is its inherent incapacity for full realization. The dynamics of the process are such that at the very moment when it seems closest to fulfillment, its achievement is spoiled by the natural inadequacies of its human personnel. American history may be seen to be moving in a cyclical fashion in which achievement is followed by crisis, to be followed again by achievement. The special significance of America is that the continuing commitment to the achievement of the country's national purpose creates often the awareness of failure and then the commitment to transform that failure into achievement again by restoring the American purpose in the light of what contemporary conditions demand. It follows from this rather distinctive relationship between national purpose and social order that the history of this country can perhaps best be understood as a continuous attempt to bring the realities of America's social and economic life into balance with the American purpose.

In this way, America's great accomplishments may be most clearly seen and appreciated. Our citizens have often diverged on the proper route to take, their disagreements contributing on occasion to national paralysis and trauma, but out of these difficult periods the nation has typically emerged with renewed faith in the belief that yet another barrier has been breached in an inexorable continuum leading toward ultimate personal fulfillment for its people and general social harmony. It should not be surprising, therefore, to discover that America's approach to the outside world has reflected this credo in all of its dimensions, including the contradictions.

As we shall note, in the unfolding of the country's history, some aspects of America's world view worked at cross-purposes with others, and a number of important ideals were adulterated in practice. Over time the nation was generally fortunate in that it was able to reduce to manageable proportions whatever contradictions existed in its world view. Thus, the country was able to operate reasonably well while dealing with its central paradoxes. Americans developed a partial accommodation of sorts between the arrival of the first settlers and the early years of the constitutional republic—an accommodation that, despite its manifest contradictions and even pathologies, was characterized by great dynamism. Later in the nineteenth century, sometimes referred to as the "formative era" of America's foreign relations, a rather clear popular consensus underlying the young nation's participation in foreign affairs became the basis for its conduct. It would not be until the twentieth century, however, that, in the midst of fleshing out its great power status, the full dimensions of these contradictions would bear fruit. The country has been living with the consequences ever since.

AMERICA'S WORLD VIEW

The American people have approached foreign policy closely bound up with a variety of tightly entangling traditions. These traditions have grown out of native American experiences and culture and have reflected certain basic characteristics of the whole of American life.[1] Taken together they may be said to constitute a view of the larger world of which America is a part.

The Impact of Geography

The geography of America, both in terms of its relative isolation from the rest of the world and in the physical characteristics of the country, has played an important role in the determination of the values of its people. Compared to the experience of any other world power in modern history, the total mix of America's geographical conditions has been rather unusual, if not singular.

The impact of geography can best be seen in terms of three conditions of the American scene: first, the long physical separation of the nation from the mainstream of world affairs—a separation that contributed both to a feeling of genuine security on the part of its people, and to their conception of living in a divided world; second, the immense size of the country, which, in terms of its shifting population, conditioned the phenomenon of the "moving frontier." It was this ubiquitous "moveable feast" that had so much to do with the evolving independence of attitude on the part of Americans and with the elaboration of America's nationalist ideology. The third geographical factor consisted of a great natural abundance that would come in time to be translated into enormous advantage.

In terms of the separation of America, the oceans played a significant role in distancing the early settlers from their homelands. This enhanced their sense of isolation from Europe and encouraged a perception of the world as being essentially a divided one. The location of America also reduced contact and removed the necessity of direct experience with the realities of international life for a very long time.

America is also the only major state in the world today without powerful neighbors. Throughout its history the consequences of its great distance from other powerful states conferred distinct benefits, whether they be the avoidance of war, the capacity to develop itself internally without danger of foreign interference, and ultimately, as its power expanded, distance from danger as a necessary corollary to its capacity to fill the role of a reserve and finally decisive force on the world stage. This was a role that America played to great advantage in two world wars. Even today, America's strategic position continues to facilitate a much wider range of policy options on substantive issues for its policy-makers than other major states customarily enjoy.

Then, too, the very size of America's hinterland contributed to the sense of security enjoyed by most of its people; preoccupation with internal challenges associated with taming the vast frontier served to insulate the typical American from the larger world. In time, this reality, reinforced as it was by the great physical gulf around its perimeters, would generate in many Americans a pervasive ignorance of the complex realities of the international milieu.

The geographical environmentalism inherent in the "frontier thesis" as explanation of American history retains, despite its flaws, considerable merit.[2] The pioneer's necessity of submitting to hardships and low living standards in the expectation of future higher standards encouraged the growth of a pervasive optimism. So also the frontier projection of the individual ahead of society and the self-reliant way of life on the edge of civilization stimulated American individualism.

A compelling factor in all of this remains that American history, through most of its course, presented a series of recurring social evolutions in diverse geographical areas as the American people advanced to colonize a continent. The major hallmark of this development in the country's attitude toward foreign affairs was the notion that the American experience was one of continuous, inexorable progress.

The great abundance to be found on America's land was, of course, something that from the beginning differentiated its development from that of Europe. The spectacle of vast riches waiting to be taken inspired successive generations of Americans to devise new means of grasping them and thus provided the necessary catalyst and context for the epic discoveries that called into being America's unparalleled technology.

It also led to a number of unwarranted assumptions on the part of its people. Americans have frequently tended to ascribe their historical good fortune and relative security to their own efforts more than sound scholarship would substantiate. The inevitable obverse of this habit has been America's propensity to minimize and distort what was occurring outside its frontiers. These tendencies, to the extent that they have prevailed, continue to encourage a relatively shallow appreciation for the roots of problems and the complex interplay of cause and effect in world affairs.

Economic Abundance

Probably the single most important environmental reality influencing the development of the American nation has been the economic richness of the vast American domain. The importance of America's wealth has rarely been questioned, and a long procession of observers have pointed to it as a basic and conspicuous feature of American life. In virtually every index of natural economic resource—cultivable soil, water, diverse minerals—abundance has characterized the historic American scene; and our material standard of living, measured in terms of more automobiles and telephones, more appliances and home entertainment centers, more swimming pools and Jacuzzis, more computers and microwave ovens, more supermarkets and movie theaters, has been generally higher than any other nation historically.

Yet what David Potter and others have called the unique "economic abundance" of America must be seen as something more than simply the great natural wealth of the nation, for the pervasive influence of abundance has impinged upon many aspects of American life that have no obvious relation to its standard of living. Most especially, it has affected America's social and political conditions, contributing in diverse ways to the shaping of its traditions.[3]

It was certainly not inevitable that succeeding generations of immigrants would be successful in transforming the natural wealth of this country into tangible social benefits. Though based upon an advantageous primary (natural) environment, America's abundance came to be realized through the creation by its people of a "secondary environment" of social abundance. The great triumph of America in this regard has been the successful translation of the one into the other. To that end, it was the particular nature of the social makeup and character of the developing American nation that was the critically important factor in that transformation—the aptitude of the society for it, and the effectiveness with which the country's resources were converted into energy and productive capacity.[4]

America's success in the conversion of its natural wealth was not a matter of simple largesse or luck. It was determined by the nation's economic free enterprise system with its emphasis upon individual initiative, and the technological advancement of the society that these values augured. It required a sequence of intervening variables (conditioning factors) to bring it off: those qualities of the general population such as its ingenuity, education, and tool skills; the nature of the "incentives" that served to energize its individual inhabitants;[5] the country's institutional framework; and, finally, what Alvin Gouldner has called the "intellectual capital" of the nation.[6] It was the genius of the American people—the struggles of the pioneer, the exertions of the working man, the pragmatic "horse sense" of the inventor, the drive of the entrepreneur, and the efficiency of all kinds of ordinary Americans who have shared a well-known addiction to hard work—that made all the difference.

The Impact of Abundance upon the American Purpose. Abundance has affected the quality of American life in many ways but nowhere more surely than in the formulation and elaboration of the American ideal and practice of equality, with all that that ideal has meant for the individual citizen in terms of opportunity to get ahead in society and to be free from a system of status.

Equality has never meant in American life an identical or even consistent arrangement on some particular social or economic plane but rather has signified a general opportunity for any person to transcend many social levels. In other words, in America equality has meant that anyone has the opportunity to get ahead, to get to the top; virtually unrestricted access in terms of social mobility has provided the underpinning for the notion of equality in America. It is in this context that the concept of freedom in America may best be understood. Freedom has been the crucial means for maintaining an open scale of opportunity. Freedom (the principle that permits one individual to be different from another) might appear to be incompatible with equality (the rule that impels the individual to be similar to others), but in America, freedom, meaning the chance to get ahead in life, and equality, implying impartiality of opportunity, have become virtually identical.[7]

Thus, the ubiquity of material abundance in American history led inevitably to the idea that equality was synonymous with equal opportunity in competition for the fruits of the marketplace. The ultimate value of equality was as a means to advancement rather than as a measurable asset in and of itself, since the idea possessed no inherent meaning except as process. As its potential value could be realized only by actual movement to a higher level, the term *equality* traditionally took on almost the same meaning that the term *upward mobility* has come to symbolize in the modern era. The national purpose of this country, elaborated in this fashion, continues to reflect these assumptions.

The Relationship with Democracy. Tocqueville put the relationship between economic abundance and democracy clearly when he said: "The chief circumstance which has favored the establishment and the maintenance of a democratic system in the United States is the nature of the territory that the Americans inhabit. Their ancestors give them the love of equality and of freedom; but God himself gave them the means of remaining equal and free by placing them upon a boundless continent."[8]

Those who have tended to see the American experience largely in terms of its political democracy have ignored the fact that in every country the system of government is in one sense a function of the social and economic conditions of life and that democracy, like any other ideology, is perhaps most appropriate for nations where the situation is congenial for it and less applicable for others with unfavorable conditions. Viewed in this way, there is a strong argument to be made that democracy is clearly most suitable for nations that enjoy a relatively high standard of living and least suitable for nations where there are gross economic deficiencies.[9]

A country with inadequate capital, for example, cannot safely provide for the bulk of its people more than security of status—at a rather primitive level in the social hierarchy and with little more than a subsistence standard of living. But that type of situation is, in its repudiation of equality, by definition, undemocratic. A democracy, on the other hand, positing equality as its most important goal, must provide opportunity, for the goal of equality becomes a travesty unless there is some manner of attaining it. Yet, in providing opportunity, a democracy is continually arousing hopes and expectations that it may lack the capacity to fulfill. In so doing, it is banking on its ability to acquire the necessary wherewithal by the very act of arousing people to demand it and pursue it. Thus, in a democracy, there is a prevailing commitment to the education of as many numbers of its community as possible, but how often is this done without waiting to see whether the appropriate jobs requiring that education are in fact available? The typical democratic state in the West will tend to do this in the expectation that the supply will create a demand and that a society continually advancing in the level of its education will inexorably generate new positions for which educated people are required.[10]

All this is very fine and works beautifully if the nation adhering to these practices possesses the requisite physical resources and human capital to hike the standard of living, to engender new occupational opportunities, and to locate outlets for the talents of an ever-proliferating class of trained citizens. If it does not, there will be trouble ahead. In a word, to prevail as a democracy, a nation must enjoy an economic surplus at the outset or must endeavor to obtain one.[11] If these observations have any validity, they suggest that the canons of democracy are not necessarily cosmic truths but, rather, that democracy is the most precious of all the many benefits that America's economic wealth has bought for its citizens. Insight into this hard truth is a prerequisite for putting into proper perspective America's historic tradition of foreign policy.

Consequences for Foreign Policy. From the beginning, it has almost been universally believed among Americans that their system of democracy, with its subsumed purpose of equality in freedom, has represented a clarion call for the rest of mankind. For many years, as Americans looked out across the vast oceans at the world locked in the remorseless vise of its own petty jealousies, they believed that their democratic "way of life" held out the ultimate salvation for the rest of mankind. To the degree that Americans have assumed that a world-wide adoption of democracy is inevitable, they have preferred to hold out their own style of democracy for others to emulate, despite their frequent contradictory behavior, confident in the belief that their own experience was ample encouragement and justification for its adoption elsewhere. This matter would come to a head in the post-1945 era in regard to the challenges posed by international communism.

Although democracy in the American manner had difficulty initially gaining ascendancy in other parts of the globe, there was a long interval extending over most of the nineteenth century during which America's ideals appeared as a beacon to the poor and destitute of the earth. Millions of these people came to America because it seemed a refuge for the oppressed, and countless others who stayed at home were uplifted by the American dream. The moral authority of America's ideals of freedom in equality and of opportunity was immense, and Americans, one supposes, were entitled to believe that for every aristocrat who disparaged them were thousands of humble men and women who shared in and were heartened by America's aspirations. The American people, desirous of the approval of others, could find comfort in the assurance that the heart of humanity seemingly responded to the creed of its democracy. This assurance went far to mitigate the disappointment at the failure of American-style democracy for many years to take firm root overseas. The twentieth century has been especially problematic for America in this regard. Few other aspects of the country's foreign policy would so clearly frustrate

Americans as their attempts over time to hold out their own democratic institutions as models for others to copy.[12]

As the American people sought to comprehend the uncertain ground of international politics as seedbed for the growth of democratic institutions during these years, the world was often not as it seemed. It was in these moments that the Puritan Ethic would come to the fore, confounding our efforts at understanding, with intolerance and inhumane action not infrequently the instinctive reaction and support for non-democratic regimes the ongoing policy.

The Puritan Ethic

The legacy of the so-called "puritan heritage" has long been held up by historians as a major contributing factor to the greatness of America.[13] The right of dissent—the belief that the individual inherently retains the privilege to agree with or to dissent from the majority if one so desires—is one of the most precious elements of that heritage; so also the notion of the dignity of human life derived from the view that man is a reflection of God and that all men are equal before their Maker. This was quite obviously an optimistic notion—a concept that argued that equality exists not simply as a potentiality in the nature of man but as an objective social reality in the unfolding of American society; a view that suggested that advantages or liabilities are not all that decisive and that every man is the architect of his own destiny. These concepts of human dignity and equality and the right of dissent did much to prepare the way within the developing American polity for the promotion of the ideas of self-determination, popular sovereignty, and the democratization of the decision-making process.

Had these been the only legacies the Puritans bequeathed to later generations, the course of American history might have been rather different. As is usual in human affairs, nothing is quite so simple. There is a darker side as well. The values handed down to the present generation of Americans by their Puritan forebears represent a complex and strange admixture of admirable qualities and retrograde orientations.

H. L. Mencken once wrote that fear and envy are the two main characteristics of Puritanism. Evidence of this he saw in the tendency of Americans to chase monsters and burn witches from the time of the British Redcoats to the Bolsheviks in the Red Scare of 1919.[14] Whatever else it was, American Puritanism was quite often fanatical and dogmatic, tending to be possessed of a strong inclination to mind other people's business.

One of the most firmly rooted attributes of the Puritan Ethic was its fundamentalism. The will of God was to be found in a literal interpretation and application of the Bible. No ecclesiastical hierarchy was necessary to reveal the truth. Such determination, it was felt, could best be ascertained by Americans themselves, for truth was immanent in things, its discovery requiring merely proper diligence and "right-living" on the part of each individual.[15]

This marked religious fundamentalist strand would lead in time to a rather powerful tradition of secular fundamentalism in the American national character—a fundamentalism still quite evident today. For one thing, it has underlain the tendency of Americans over the years to reduce complex real-life situations to basic, black-and-white formulations. Because many of America's first settlers—and indeed, its later waves of immigrants—had either been persecuted for their way of life or disadvantaged by the social systems in which they had lived, they naturally tended to reduce the reasons for their alienation to relatively primitive, unsophisticated explanations. The tendency of Americans to pinpoint "first causes" for their travails thus came to pass.

The developing American fondness for reducing reality to the simplicity of hallowed slogans would come to haunt us during and after World War II, betraying an insufficient grasp of the historical, political, and socioeconomic processes with which foreign policy must deal. For the true believer, emphasis on complexity represents an infuriating affront to his sense of simple fundamentalist perspective. Fundamentalist faith provides people with yardsticks (however crude) and solutions to problems (however irrational) that Americans have often found comforting and irresistible. Delusions of power and of the truth are clearly rooted in the fundamentalist absolutism of the historic Puritan Ethic–attributes that would plague America in its dealings with Soviet Russia.

Perhaps the most unsavory aspect of America's Puritan legacy has been our tendency to personify problems. A view that developed early within the Puritan communities was one in which it was thought the world was a battleground where good and evil forces fought one another. Devils and witches were everywhere, causing thunderstorms, strangling infants in their cradles, making people ill, sinking ships, and ruining crops. For the Puritan, battles with these villains were necessarily proper and righteous. As objective conflicts of interest did not exist, any prolonged disagreement inevitably tended to lead one to question the motives and morality of the person or group doing the disagreeing. Americans have long exhibited a distressing tendency to search for scapegoats for their problems. When the going gets tough, they frequently push the moral panic button, thrashing about in their frustration and rage, seeking to fix blame for their momentary reverses on those within the community whose "impure thoughts" are responsible for the most unwelcome reverses.[16]

Denis Brogan once remarked that "the illusion of American omnipotence" has given rise to the belief that "any situation which distresses or endangers the United States can only exist because some Americans have been fools or knaves."[17] Since the assumptions on which the policies of true believers are based are adjudged to be correct and the principles right, fiasco must be attributed to devils. Because a normal world, by definition devoid of such monsters, is in harmony, the postponement of bliss must be due to unscrupulous characters. American foreign policy has paid a fearful price for such beliefs, most especially in the many missed opportunities for peaceful conflict management that characterized its Cold War relationship with the Russian state.[18]

Distrust of Power. Another characteristic of the Puritan Ethic deserves special mention: a long-time, deep-seated distrust of power, whatever the source. The Puritans developed the notion early on that a struggle for power is not a proper basis for the moral life. Their misgivings may be traced to what the Puritans felt was the abuse of power and of the conception of responsibility by both the ecclesiastical and secular authorities in England and on the European continent in the sixteenth and seventeenth centuries. It is significant that both the Plymouth Company and the Massachusetts Bay Colony were chartered and settled in the midst of the Protestant Reformation and the Thirty Years War. Was it any wonder that for these people war was viewed as immoral, unjust, and illegal? To this end, the Puritan Ethic, in its simplest statement, says that "somehow, some way, right will prevail over might." The Mayflower Compact in this vein illustrates the dichotomy of the struggle between the religious and temporal realms and the attempt to develop some third alternative where America's first iconoclasts could better order, preserve, and further their own ends.

Distrust of power has influenced a number of important developments in American history. On the personal level, it contributed to a rather strong egalitarianism and rugged individualism. On the national level, we see it woven into the Constitution of 1789 with its elaborate system of checks and balances, whereby none of the three major branches of government would be invested with absolute sovereignty.

On the international level, America's corrosive doubts about the concept has been typified in the form of aspersion of so-called power politics, spheres of influence and balances of power. There is no question that the politics of power, viewed as the immoral and avaricious pursuit of goals and objectives by any and all means, has generated in Americans a profound distaste. In this sense, as a country whose passage through history may be seen as the vindication of the Puritan Ethic, it was perfectly natural for the American nation to categorically repudiate power politics as a violation of the moral life. The perceived scorn shown frequently by foreign political leaders toward moral uprightness and their seeming habit of choosing the expedient over the ethical have often violated the consciences of Americans, leading them to seek morally defensible postures upon which to predicate the country's behavior in the world.

Cultural Diversity and Parochialism

The particular manner in which America was constituted—cultural diversity interacting with unmatched economic abundance—has also exerted a great influence on the country's historical outlook. America is the only major state in the world today whose people, originating from other lands, occupied an extensive, highly endowed, and sparsely settled land mass. No where else does one find an example of a country with a large population whose forebears came primarily from elsewhere, which has emulated the American experience of homogenizing a multitude of people from many backgrounds into one nation enjoying great material benefits and a high standard of living.

Consider the implications of this novel situation. People of many backgrounds came to America, labored side by side on free and plentiful land, in a context in which (the slaves and Indians excepted) man was not relegated to a permanently inferior status by accident of birth. Consider, further, the inevitable effects of this great amalgam of cultures in a largely unfenced, underdeveloped land, in which many of the problems to be faced had no conventional or traditional solution. Captain John Smith at Jamestown (1607) got right to the point: "He who does not work, neither shall he eat."

Two facts about this situation were crucial: First, it involved novel problems for which European customs possessed no really appropriate or translatable formulas; and second, peoples from diverse European cultures retained their own unique predetermined answers to problems. Thus, a relatively classless society constructed from the interaction of multiple cultural influences was elaborated within the "clean slate" components of an environmental arrangement where power and authority flowed virtually not at all from custom. This cultural diversity, obtained in the fashion that it was, has had at least three consequences for America's approach to foreign policy.

First, while "America is an impressively capable society, we are also," as Edmund Stillman and William Pfaff have noted, "a peculiarly parochial society with a poor record of deep or comprehensive interest in other societies."[19] Perhaps one reason for this has been the intensity of the American national experience—the necessity Americans have felt historically to concentrate upon making themselves into a nation. The states of Europe, after all, became modern nations by building upon their own already existing social commonalities. The American people, on the other hand, represent an extraordinary collection of human beings from virtually everywhere. One might suppose that America's worldwide origins would have generated among its people an understanding of or, at least, an affinity for others. Such has not been the case.

A contributing factor to this lack of identity with other peoples has been the fact that Americans have tended to be insulated from the primary locus of international life. Most of the people living in this country were born and raised in an environment relatively untouched by foreign influences and unencumbered by any major concerns about the nature or direction of other societies.[20] Thus, insensitive to the significance and impact of cultural diversity, Americans have tended to appraise the world in terms of their own unique cultural criteria—a historical inclination that Charles Lerche once called a "dominant cultural particularism."[21]

Then, too, their peculiar cultural experience has quite naturally led successive generations of Americans to turn inward in an all-encompassing concern with their internal development. The historic emphasis on the domestic side of politics is certainly understandable. From their earliest moments, Americans were more preoccupied with protecting themselves from a hostile environment, carving out new portions of the wilderness, or making a living than they were with the complexities of international politics. Even with the closing of the seemingly limitless frontier after 1890 (Alaska notwithstanding), the absorption in domestic affairs and the pursuit of material wealth has remained a well-established pattern of thinking.

Second, a nation created *e pluribus unum* ("from many, one") may be excused if it is led to believe that its people think like all, since they were derived from all. Yet, the realities of the American historical experience meant the many were intermingled under geographical, economic, and social conditions that made them emblematic of none.[22] This situation, while rather apparent from a rational perspective, had led Americans as a people to confuse their unique experience with the realities of the rest of mankind. We shall examine the implications of this point in greater detail in the next chapter.

Third, from the 1880s to the 1920s some forty million immigrants settled in America, largely as a result of the great deprivations and cultural conflicts that characterized many European nations during these years.[23] While in some sense these endemic conflicts were beneficial in that they helped to prevent the European powers from uniting to America's detriment, they also made it extremely difficult for an incumbent American administration to formulate policies toward European affairs that commanded a high degree of national unity. For a long time, the only policy likely to gain widespread support among most major ethnic minorities in America was isolationism, by whose canons the nation refrained altogether from intervening in Europe's political controversies. To this day, the presence of immigrant groups in the nation has constituted a bona fide tangible variable for sitting presidents—one that does not normally contribute to rational policy-making in the national interest.

Moralism

Perhaps the most characteristic of America's earliest European inhabitants, and later, most consonant with its general position in the world, has been the technique of appealing to the common sense and goodwill of those with whom it has come into contact. The notion of equality in freedom taught that human beings are possessed of reason and morality and that they will respond to calls couched in those terms. Americans have, therefore, attempted to carve out positions that can be defended on ethical grounds and to employ these norms in their dealings with other states.[24]

The earliest Americans were habitually inclined to invest their ongoing struggles to survive and prosper in America, with all the attendant disputes and divergencies of such contentions, with a deep moralist coloration.[25] This moralist conception came over time to imply an abstract, transcendent, ethical norm—the belief that there is a fundamental difference between right and wrong; that right must be supported, that wrong must be suppressed, and that error and evil can have no place when compared with the "truth." This conception eventually took on the guise of a kind of golden rule by which everything else was to be measured. It could and did retain its imperative quality without reference to whether or not it could be translated into political practice or, indeed, whether it even corresponded to reality. More important from the perspective of foreign policy, it was a norm that from the beginning had messianic implications, although for a long time it was viewed primarily as the basis for developing and securing the "new society" at home.

In America's case, the core of its moralist approach to reality has been a tendency to find one theme to encapsulate a central evil that is thought to dominate "our time," then commit ourselves to all-out war against it. Resort to such themes in the context of the nation's fundamentalist propensity has often amounted to generating maxims out of moral principles that are easily corrupted into simple catchwords.

Such a single-factor approach tends to partake of an illusory simplicity, whether its object has been, internally, the threat of communists in government or, externally, the peril of "falling dominoes." This approach has often had the effect of creating a situation where anyone who opposed America was, according to Americans, a "bad" (e. g., irrational-immoral) person, thereby generating in us a better frame of mind to prosecute the inevitable ensuing struggle. More specifically, America's strident moralism would contribute to the adoption of unrealistic and even destructive policies in its foreign relations in the years after its entry into the Second World War. "Unconditional surrender," "total victory," "no appeasement," and "better dead than Red" are illustrative of the sorts of postures that were encouraged by the self-delusions of the moralist impulse.

The Thrust Toward Harmony

America, Stanley Hoffmann has reminded us, "is a nation impatient with, intolerant of, unaccustomed and unadjusted to basic conflicts of ends."[26] The intellectual roots of this attitude go deep into the recesses of American history. The immigrants who established and settled America were refugees from cultures where such conflicts were often severe and unrelenting; indeed, America's "huddled masses" were often the casualties of these conflicts. It was only natural that they would desire to construct a new society of harmony and consensus. Moreover, the immigrants who came to constitute America were so diverse that this "New Jerusalem" could thrive only if their diversities necessitated the melting pot. In any society endangered by great division yet impelled toward unity, unanimity of outlook must be engendered and maintained as the only method of maintaining cohesiveness. In this way, the thrust toward harmony may be seen in American history as avoidance of the hard reality of inevitable conflict and thus in marked contrast to the perceived conditions of international affairs.

The American predilection for harmony and consensus in its social fabric has also had another root—America's fear of power politics. According to Arnold Wolfers, "America's . . . domestic political conditions stand in striking contrast to the conditions [other] nations face in their external relations; the domestic conditions are characterized by order, lawfulness and peace arising from popular consensus on principle—a consensus so marked that some believe coercion has practically ceased to play a role here; but the external relations continue to be full of bitter struggle, violence, and Machiavellian practices."[27]

A deep rigidity on this point, puritanical in its obduracy, early became an ingrained trait among Americans, one that would manifest itself in many guises throughout the nation's history. The impatience of Americans with what they have perceived as "wrongdoing" on the part of others has often been insensitive and at times sanctimonious. Insofar as it is part of the American experience to expect harmony as the norm, consensus is felt to be by Americans not only possible among nations as the outcome of mutual adjustments among men of goodwill but also the best basis on which leaders can make choices. Anything less than this has tended to produce in Americans at the very least a marked sense of discomfort and, not infrequently, a burning desire to set things right. It is no accident that Americans would come sooner or later to the view that they were "God's avenging angels" on earth whose sacred duty it has been to combat evil philosophies. In their great desire to see the norms of consensus prevail, Americans have felt compelled to involve themselves in the world in the name of proportion, concord, and harmony.

The major problem inherent in America's thrust toward harmony is its denial that the human condition is one of ambiguity, of conflict over values visualized as ends, and among the means to those ends. The struggle for meaning, recognition, and security is an endless one. In international affairs no less than in the domestic lives of peoples, common purpose is rare, myths are many. Misperception and misunderstanding are the rule in a world in which there are almost no unifying purposes that serve to bind human beings to one another. These are the bottom lines that Americans have long been unwilling to accept.

Because of a deeply ingrained faith in the efficacy of solutions and in the inevitability of progress, Americans in particular are dismayed by those who speak of interminable problems and endless conflict. The universality of problems is simply the one fact of life Americans most persistently oppose and seek to refute by dogmas and myths. The idea of toughing it out, of treading water, or buying time is utterly incomprehensible for the American mind. Historically, Americans seem to need to have a feeling of going somewhere and accomplishing something. Above all, if life has persistent problems, it must be the system or someone else who is to blame.

It is only in this context that one can put into proper perspective the phenomenon of anti-communism as America's dominant ideology after World War II. Anti-communism arose from the frustrations of the early postwar period. To possess a military power unequaled in human history, to have marshaled a nuclear arsenal capable of eradicating an enemy in a matter of days, to have no conscious political ambitions other than to make the world safe for America's business and to make the virtues of American democracy available to less fortunate peoples—to experience all this and still not be able to achieve more than a stalemate in its contest with Soviet Russia for over four decades would prove to be very, very difficult for many Americans to accept. The transformation of adversaries into demons followed almost inevitably.[28]

Not long after the Cold War had been set in concrete, Walter Lippmann wrote a piece in which he commented upon America's basic dislike and misunderstanding of conflict in human affairs. The tendency, he said, has filled American foreign policy with "stereotyped prejudices and sacred cows and wishful conceptions." The basic failure of American conceptual thinking in foreign policy, he went on, is "to admit that rivalry and strife and conflict among states, communities and factions are the normal condition of mankind."[29] In this nation trusting mightily in persuasion, goodwill, moral exhortation, majority votes, and the rule of law, it is only natural for Americans to have tended to underestimate as a people the impact of interest on the minds and actions of people and nations while yet overestimating the harmony that is actual and possible among those interests.

The Self-Image of Uniqueness

The American people came to the view early in their experience that they were an exceptional people, unlike any other and therefore not liable for evaluation according to normal standards of behavior. It was essentially American history itself, both before and after 1789, that led Americans to the conclusion that they were unique. No one has been quite like us, and it is not proper to ask that we conduct ourselves like anyone else. It should not then be surprising that the foreign policy role of America would come to be conceived of as qualitatively distinct from that of any other country.

In looking at what evidence exists of life in colonial America, one detects an ever-expanding sense of this self-image of uniqueness on the part of its people.[30] The pre-Revolutionary concept of uniqueness was thoroughly infused with religious exultation. John Winthrop stated as early as 1630, "Men shall say of succeeding plantacions [sic]: the Lord shall be as a City upon a Hill, the eies [sic] of all people upon us." Throughout the colonial period, one sees continual references to the notion that the "Great God" himself was shining down upon the American people in all his beneficence. An act of divine Providence was making possible the opportunity for Americans to build together a truly just and God-fearing society.[31]

America's demonstrated sense of aloofness from the international arena also contributed to the assertion of the dogma of uniqueness in American history. The distinctions between America and other nations come to be viewed in the popular mind as yardsticks by means of which foreigners usually came up short of the country's own moral standards. Morality became the reference point of uniqueness; Americans were simply "better" than the common run-of-the-mill peoples of the world whose flaws Americans would put up with but never countenance.

There was additionally a strong secular element in this aspect of the American consciousness. The Declaration of Independence was itself a great contributing factor to generating a powerful sense of special worth among Americans. The assumption of many colonists that they were purifying the very special tradition of the "rights of free Englishmen" enhanced their awareness of being unique.[32] One sees echoes of this perception in Washington's Farewell Address: "Our detached and distant position," he said, "invites us and enables us to pursue a different course from that of the states of Europe." The shift toward the secular argument became more pronounced with the formulation and adoption of the Constitution. Many Americans considered the theory and substance of that great document to involve a true innovation in the political history of humankind. "Before the establishment of the American states," Jefferson said, "nothing was known to history but the man of the Old World, crowded within limits either small or overcharged, and stuped in the vices which that situation generates."[33]

As the nineteenth century wore on, increasing numbers of Americans were reasoning that God himself intended to divide the globe into separate spheres. America was the "new Zion," and Providence had secured this "American Israel" from a time-worn, corrupt, and warring continent. But about the time of the war against Mexico in 1846, one begins to detect a substantive change in the self-image; the concept of uniqueness comes to be invoked not only as a confident explanation of America's special nature but also as a justification for actions that seemed clearly to violate other values and ideals inherent in the American national experience.

Being unusual, and this hallmark of distinctiveness being made most clearly manifest by the nation's moral preeminence, it was only a short step for Americans to aver that they should be evaluated by special criteria—a singular set of standards qualitatively different than those applied to other countries. In this way, actions not permitted other peoples became perfectly acceptable when undertaken by America. In December 1848, President James Polk, fresh from his conquests of Mexico, could say: "Our blessed country presents a sublime spectacle to the world."

Conversely, forms of state action, regarded as perfectly permissible by the international system at the time, were by definition barred to Americans. Power politics continued to be seen as immoral; Americans would never engage in it, no matter how common the practice might be among other countries. How, then, was the country to rationalize its acquisition of empire during the course of the nineteenth century? The answer was not long in coming: It was not "imperialistic" for America to grab overseas territories, since American purposes were disinterested and public-spirited; America would take care of these "unfortunates" in its own good manner.

From the days of Manifest Destiny to the era of the American Century, the foreign policy of the nation would be evocative of this sense of uniqueness. When the time came during the Second World War for America to play a major role in world politics, its long history of self-indulgence in this regard would serve it poorly indeed. From that moment, America's self-image of uniqueness tended to center around what many of its leading policy-makers called its "world responsibility." Not long after he assumed the presidency, Harry Truman asserted that "all the world knows that the fate of civilization depends, to a very large extent, on what we do." In early 1947, Hanson Baldwin, military editor of the *New York Times*, wrote that "the United States is the key to the destiny of tomorrow. We alone may be able to avert the decline of Western civilization, and a reversion to nihilism and the Dark Ages." Almost twenty years later, in the midst of the Vietnam War, Lyndon Johnson observed at a Lincoln Day dinner that "History and our own achievements have thrust upon us the principal responsibility for the protection of freedom on earth. For the next ten or twenty years, the burden will be placed completely on our country for the preservation of freedom."[34]

These sorts of statements reflected at one and the same time an evocation of the exceptionalness of America and the view that others, being morally stunted, naturally required its assistance. According to its most articulate spokespersons, what was most required in the post-1945 world was the construction of a framework for a new era of righteous peace. This America was eminently equipped to provide. After all, America was an example of a successful revolution, uncompromised by an imperialist past or a history of self-centered policies. Americans were uniquely qualified to lead the forces of freedom since there was no one else to take up this burden. The states of Europe were weak by contemporary standards of power, and most of them were morally unqualified since they were compromised by histories of colonial exploitation and selfish nationalism. What is more, they were ill-equipped to teach democracy because their own records of democracy were so poor. In the struggle with tyranny, they did not have clean hands.[35]

Today Americans continue to like to hear that the nation is exceptional and should not be judged by the criteria applied to other countries. Possessed of surpassing talents and an exceptional history, we are still prone to employ the same sort of reasoning that led Abraham Lincoln to declare that this nation is "the last best hope of earth." There is simply no reason why the rest of the world, with America's help and experience, should not similarly compose itself to a life without sordid self-interest and violent conflict. In this way, the substance of America's self-image has been seen to be appropriate for all, our talents now at last recognized as relevant for all people, our virtues no longer merely the virtues of America but the virtues of all the world. George Ball captured the official altruism of America in these words: "[N]ever before in human history has a nation undertaken to play a role of world responsibility except in defense and support of a world empire. We find ourselves in a position unique in world history."[36]

It should now be rather evident that this country's self-image of uniqueness is as elusive to others as it is plain to its own people. The incredible self-righteousness of many Americans in this regard has only engendered resentment and criticism from others. Despite its considerable justification, such criticism provokes frustration and outrage among the country's policy-makers. Nothing angers Americans more than second-guessing their motives—for example, the notion that Americans behave as great powers have always tended to behave: out of self-interest. In their eyes, while America may well make a mess of things, and in the process be forced to employ means as ugly as its opponents, it is redeemed in the end because "its cause is higher, its heart purer, its intent better."

For a long while Americans overlooked the ethical trap they were laying for themselves by the advocacy of this double standard. The threat of nuclear holocaust engendered by the long Russian-American confrontation after 1945 would point up the paradox and dilemma inherent in America's continual assertion of uniqueness. But in Vietnam we discovered that our constant evocation of uniqueness and moral superiority prepared the way for the disastrous doctrine that the ends always justify the means. Today many Americans are wrestling with the issues posed by this dilemma but have yet to resolve them in such a way that satisfies both the requirements of effective policy and the insistent promptings of their consciences.

The Record of Environmental Transformation

If there has been one persistent measure by which Americans and others have evaluated the performance of this nation, it is the accomplishments of its people over many years in harnessing and transforming the physical environment in which they have lived. It is no exaggeration to picture American history in this regard as the success story of human history. In terms of the triumphs of its people in breaking down the many barriers of the North American wilderness, in translating the vast resources of their landscape into the fruits of an industrial society, the likes of which the world has never before seen, America has been the marvel of the ages.

The historical details of this performance are well known and need not detain us here. Suffice it to say that within a space of some 200 years a relatively primitive agrarian society was transformed into the leading industrial giant of the earth in a framework that permitted the ingenuity and intelligence of Americans to act freely, without undue direction. As many observers have noted, the spirit of individual initiative in human enterprise was the key to the nation's hugely successful efforts to master its surroundings. There was neither a forced labor of its people (the black slaves excepted) nor even extensive government involvement in the means of production. As the first Americans struggled against the challenges posed by nature, the initial conquests were won by the plowshare. Later, as the American people fleshed out their national existence "from sea to shining sea," the country's "great leap forward" was accomplished in a milieu in which the forces of the marketplace were more free to facilitate the developmental process than in virtually any other country on earth. That process has continued apace to the point where today America, when viewed in materialist terms, is perceived by many to be the "number one nation on earth."

A key aspect of the American experience, then, from the Puritans to the space age, has been its record of mastering nature. This catalog of progress, achieved by means of no easy shortcuts but through the "blood, sweat, and tears" of countless millions of its citizens, has served to confirm in Americans the view that they are indeed exceptional; no one, it seems, has ever accomplished that Americans have done and in so short a time. It is this remarkable success story which has been responsible for a number of important cultural beliefs concerning the essence of human conduct—attitudes that in terms of America's foreign relations have been both a great asset and a source of serious difficulty for its people.

First and on the positive side, it is because Americans have achieved so much themselves that they tend to believe that progress is a normal condition in human affairs. Because they have been able to adapt in so many creative ways to the challenges of their own environment, their own history has not been so disheartening; and because they have had relatively little tragedy in their history, they remain optimistic about the future. Indeed America's historical record in this regard has tended to promote in its people a feeling that they can do anything: "The impossible takes a little longer, that's all."

Second, the catalog of America's accomplishments in environmental restructuring has meant that the kind of struggle for the control of man reflective of other societies has not been a permanent or dominating quality of American life. There has been enough stimulation in America's surroundings to shove the struggle for human control onto the "back burner," to the edge of consciousness. Until recently, America's preoccupation and great success in dealing with the manifold challenges of its natural environment have served to defuse and detoxify the more disruptive and explosive aspects inherent in the human condition in this country. This record is seen to be in marked contrast to what has been the case elsewhere.[37]

Third, in America the realities of its liberal free enterprise society guaranteed what might be called a "pure triumph of technology," unfettered by the political and social handicaps that tend to inhibit its growth or warp its realization elsewhere. In this way America's historic approach to life has been inspired by the engineer's standard of operation. In a society in which a consensus on social values indicates the ends to which individuals ought to aspire—for example, equality in freedom, self-determination, correct moral behavior, the pursuit of prosperity—it is only necessary to obtain one's goals by means that have received the stamp of certainty through the tried-and-true social methods the American people have employed historically to great success. The practical implication is clear: America is a society whose great achievement has meant mechanization, industrialization, and the arrangement of labor in the most efficient way. But when carried into the outer world, this experience has been found wanting, for, alas, the rest of humankind has not necessarily always seen it that way.

America's Isolation in Time

America has until recently defied time. From the outset, America's self-image of uniqueness generated a particularly disturbing kind of isolation in the American character—what William Appleman Williams has called "isolation in time."[38] The conviction of exceptionalness and moralist conception of reality inevitably generated in the American people a deep sense of lonely isolation. This fact can be more easily appreciated if one remembers that one of the central ingredients in America's early national experience was the idea that time was abolished for God's country. Lifted out of history, free from a limiting past, Americans were presumably more self-determining than any other national people had ever been and consequently better able to manipulate historical time for their own purposes.

Even before the Revolution, American colonists begin to repudiate the past. The ideological and psychological components of the sense of isolation were initially reinforced by geography and the time lag in communications with the nations of Europe. And as the gulf widened between Americans and their European forebears across the sea, the citizens of the "new utopia" increasingly saw little of value in anybody else, be it the French, Spanish, Russians, North Africans, or even the British.

The mythology surrounding the gestation and implementation of the Constitution also contributed to this feeling of great psychosocial isolation. By defining themselves as unique and therefore isolated, the Revolutionary Fathers in a sense lost their own awareness and perspective of history and of process. There is no question that they had carefully studied history, perhaps more than any other generation of Americans, but in cutting themselves off from their past both physically and psychologically, they became trapped in the present. In a sense, one may say that America's forefathers killed time (and history) in the name of uniqueness.[39] By concluding that the past was bad, America's founders personified a type of dynamism that was based on *"a conception of the future as the present*—as more of the same without any fundamental alterations."[40] Later, as the industrial revolution in Europe underscored the backwardness and weakness of America's agrarian-commercial political economy, that disparity would be overcome ultimately in a way that confirmed the early feelings of uniqueness, moral superiority, and aloneness. For as America replaced Britain as the world's greatest industrial power, it experienced the isolation of superiority, just as it had earlier suffered the isolation of irrelevance.

What all of this leaves one with is a feeling that America's existential activity in the world long ago became and remains today one of preserving the present indefinitely. The American tendency to discount the weight of the past is the "sign of a society which reads its own history as a kind of long prologue to the present and to the future; whose long isolation has meant that the history of others has been learned, rather than experienced."[41] It is this sort of outlook that leaves America rather short of an appreciation for the perennial aspects of the human predicament, and deficient in an understanding of the long roots of things. In the final analysis, we cannot escape history—neither that of our own nor, as it turned out, that of the Russian people with whom fate would place us during and after the Second World War.

SUMMARY: THROUGH A GLASS DARKLY

America is a vast and geographically diverse country, the settlement of which produced a natural pluralism. Throughout American history, the land and the uses to which it has been put have given rise to many competing and conflicting interests within the domestic environment. It has been the genius of America in its internal arrangements that these disagreements, honest and deeply felt, have been subordinated to a great drive for consensus and harmony in American history. In a land blessed with great natural wealth, and the human energy to activate it, participation in the building of the new society was regarded as a privilege, a right, and a necessity. Freedom in equality meant equal access and equal opportunity, and this idea sent echoes around the world. More important, it stirred people from all walks of life to crave participation in the governance of society. Tocqueville touched upon these crucial ingredients of America's democratic ethos when he wrote: "To take a hand in the regulation of society and to discuss it is his highest concern. [If] an American were condemned to confine his activities to his own affairs he would be robbed of one half of his existence."[42] Participation was a response to optimism and hope—qualities that Americans possessed in abundance.

For Benjamin Franklin "the truth [was] that there are in this country few people so miserable as the poor of Europe . . . very few that in Europe would be called rich. There are few great proprietors of the soil, and few tenants; most people cultivate their own lands, or follow some handicraft or merchandise; very few are rich enough to live idly upon their rents or incomes."[43] It did not matter much that such expressions belied the distinctions between free man and slaves, the rich and the poor, talent and mediocrity. What gave these sorts of statements credibility was the belief that history itself was being changed, that the "new American" was not a prisoner of the past, and that here, finally, was a new dispensation in which there were neither permanent overlords nor a permanent underclass.

The founders of the Republic and those who were "present at the creation" had little reason to doubt they were on the verge of producing a new glory of the ages. There was only the hard work to be done, and great accomplishments lay ahead. And, most revealing of all in terms of the self-image, was that these affirmations seemed confirmed by the first century-and-a-half of the nation's history. The moving frontier and the later technological revolution provided appropriate outlets for the adventurous and ambitious. The lucky coincidence of geographic isolation and Britain's role in the European balance of power liberated the young nation from the burdens and complexities of international responsibility. In such a world it was tempting to believe that a new and less troubled stage in history had been attained and that progress was inexorable. The end of the journey was embodied in the beginning; hope and optimism firmly grounded in a utopia already in the process of being attained.

Unhappily the reality would turn out somewhat differently. The twentieth century would see an America saddled with the burdens of leadership. Most disconcerting of all, many of the nation's most cherished values and principles would be found to be disembodied: Insofar as our norms have been grounded in political and social realities, it has often been only in that of our own. What is more, as America was forced to turn its face to an often confusing, disagreeable, and threatening world, not a few of the policy imperatives that it derived from its principles would come to confound its national purpose. As we now turn to a review of America's habits of action in the world, one conclusion is inescapable: The country's style would come more often than not to be the substance of its policy.

NOTES

1. There are many excellent studies that have detailed the unfolding of this tradition in a more strict chronological sence. Among the best diplomatic histories are those by Thomas A. Bailey, *A Diplomatic History of the American People*, 8th ed. (New York: Appleton-Century-Crofts, 1969); Samuel Flagg Bemis, *A Diplomatic History of the United States*, 5th ed. (New York: Holt, Rinehart and Winston, Inc., 1965); Lloyd C. Gardner, Walter F. LeFeber, and Thomas J. McCormick, *The Creation of the American Empire: United States Diplomatic History* (Chicago: Rand McNally, 1973); Richard W. Leopold, *The Growth of American Foreign Policy* (New York: Alfred A. Knopf, 1962); Julius W. Pratt, *A History of United States Foreign Policy*, 3rd ed. (Englewood Cliffs, N.J.: Prentice-Hall, 1972); and William Appleman Williams, ed., *The Shaping of American Diplomacy* (Chicago: Rand McNally, 1956). One of the most useful collections of documents is that of Daniel M. Smith, ed., *Major Problems in American Diplomatic History* (Boston: D. C. Heath & Co., 1964).

2. The so-called frontier thesis, associated with the writings of Frederick Jackson Turner, has come under attack in the years since Turner first propounded it, subjected to detailed analysis by such well-known historians as Charles Beard, Louis Hacker, and Henry Nash Smith to the point where few, if any, serious students of American history today would accept uncritically the entire theory. For Turner's

original exposition, see his "Contributions of the West to American Democracy," in *The Frontier in American History* (New York: Henry Holt and Co., 1920). For a bibliography of the literature on the impact of the frontier in the nation's past, which includes references to Turner's precursors, his influence, his thought, and his method, see Ray Allen Billington, *Westward Expansion* (New York: Macmillan, 1949), esp. pp. 760–761.

    3. See, for example, Henry Bamford Parkes, *The American Experience* (New York: Alfred A. Knopf, 1947); Eric F. Goldman, *Rendezvous with Destiny* (New York: Alfred A. Knopf, 1953); and Henry Steele Commager, *America in Perspective: The United States through Foreign Eyes* (New York: Mentor Books, 1948).

    4. David Potter is one of the most eloquent of those who have articulated this point of view. In his own words, in *People of Plenty* (Chicago: University of Chicago Press, 1954): "If abundance is to be properly understood, it must not be visualized in terms of a storehouse of fixed and universally recognizable assets, reposing on shelves until humanity, by a process of removal, strips all the shelves bare. Rather, abundance resides in a series of physical potentialities, which have never been inventoried at the same value for any two cultures. [It] is as a physical and cultural factor, involving the interplay between man . . . which holds different meanings for every different human culture," (p. 164).

    5. In the case of America, there is little question that it has been individualistic incentives, more than those emanating from any other quarter, that have been the driving force behind its people and their prosperity. See, in this vein, Walt W. Rostow, *The Process of Economic Growth* (New York: W. W. Norton & Co., 1952), p. 18, in which the onetime MIT economic historian argues that the subject of economic abundance and growth should be studied within a framework of the human or social propensities that "summarize the effective response of a society to its environment at any given period of time."

    6. Alvin Gouldner avers in "Prologue to a Theory of Revolutionary Intellectuals," *TELOS*, No. 26 (Winter, 1975–1976), pp. 3–36, that the role of intellectuals in any society is crucial in its development, for their privileges and influence are grounded in their education, knowledge, culture, and language, which they, in turn, are largely responsible for disseminating and legitimizing.

    7. Potter, *People of Plenty*, p. 92.

    8. Alexis de Tocqueville, *Democracy in America*, ed., Phillips Bradley (New York: Vintage Books, 1958), 1, p. 137.

    9. There are, of course, a handful of exceptions in the contemporary world, India being the most prominent. The case of India demonstrates the importance of other variables, for example, the impact of the British colonial service, in influencing a country's political development.

    10. Potter, *People of Plenty*, p. 116.

    11. Ibid.

    12. This is not to say, of course, that there have not been conspicuous successes. The idiosyncratic cases of Japan and the Federal Republic of Germany immediately come to mind. In those two cases, however, a determined policy of democratization was able to be successfully imposed on two societies devastated by war.

    13. From the perspective of the development of human civilization, Puritanism may be best thought of as a manifestation of what Louis Hartz has called

the "general liberal movement in Western history." Puritanism was a theological formulation of certain ideas that ultimately in a secular form became the basis of America's political liberalism. The Declaration of Independence in this sense is a Puritan document.

In the unfolding of Western history, there occurred a historical transition from the medieval world into the world of secular liberal values we know today. The most important vehicle for that transformation was the Protestant Reformation and its various individualistic derivatives. Puritanism was part and parcel of that process. There were certain intrinsic ideas in the non-conformist religious movements of the sixteenth and seventeenth centuries that, detaching themselves from their more overtly religious aspects, entered into much more human formulations and became integral aspects of the mainstream of modern Western political development.

For an in-depth discussion of this Western liberal tradition, see Louis Hartz, *The Liberal Tradition in America: An Interpretation of American Political Thought since the Revolution* (New York: Harcourt, Brace and World, 1955).

14. H. L. Mencken, *Notes on Democracy* (New York: John Putnam & Sons, 1926), p. 27.

15. For the notion of America living a purposeful unfolding of the truths developed by the Puritans and later personified by the Founding Fathers, see Daniel J. Boorstin, *The Genius of American Politics* (Chicago: University of Chicago Press, 1953).

16. It was the Puritans, after all, who burned unbelievers as witches in Salem, Massachusetts, and drove Roger Williams, a leading dissenter, out of the Massachusetts Bay Colony. Williams had argued that the Puritan leaders had no right to punish people for their religious beliefs. There were two periods of witch-hunting in New England in the seventeenth century: from 1647 to 1663 and from 1688 to 1693. In the end, the witch-hunt frenzy became so irrational that even some leaders of Puritan communities were accused of being witches. Very quickly thereafter, the hysteria subsided.

17. Denis W. Brogan, "The Illusion of American Omnipotence," *Harpers* 205 (December, 1952), pp. 21–28. See also his *American Aspects* (New York: Harper & Row, 1964), esp. Chapter 2.

18. For the impact of Puritanism on the country's approach to the outer world, see David L. Larson, *The Puritan Ethic in U.S. Foreign Policy* (New York: Van Nostrand, 1966).

19. Edmund Stillman and William Pfaff, *Power and Impotence* (New York: Vintage Books, 1966), p. 44.

20. This characterization, of course, has never been valid concerning much of the Jewish population of the country, nor about dozens of other immigrant groups (e. g., Mexicans) who continue for one reason or another to maintain interest in, contact with, and support for a wide variety of outside communities. And with the more recent arrivals of Vietnamese, Cubans, and Haitians in America, some sections of the country (e. g., New York, Florida, Texas, and California) have taken on the atmosphere of foreign enclaves. Nevertheless, the impact of these newer arrivals, with the exception of the Cuban community, has not yet been felt very much, either in the bureaucracy of the foreign policy-making process or even in the Congress, where one would expect the influence to show up first. The prevailing value norms are still derived from "middle America."

21. Charles O. Lerche, Jr., *Foreign Policy of the American People*, 3rd ed. (Englewood Cliffs, N.J.: Prentice-Hall, 1967), p. 108.

22. Frederick H. Hartmann, *The New Age of American Foreign Policy* (New York: Macmillan, 1970), p. 42, makes this point.

23. See J. Joseph Huthmacher, *A Nation of Newcomers: Ethnic Minority Groups in American History* (New York: Dell, 1967), p. 7.

24. For an excellent treatment of the American preference for moral techniques, see the article by Hans J. Morgenthau, "The Mainsprings of American Foreign Policy: The National Interest vs. Moral Abstractions," *American Political Science Review* (December, 1950), pp. 833–854. See also Adrienne Koch, *Power, Morals and the Founding Fathers: Essays on the Interpretation of the American Enlightenment* (Ithaca, N.Y.: Great Seal Books, 1961). It is also worth reading J. William Fulbright's critique of American moralism in the context of Russian-American relations, as developed at length in his *Old Myths and New Realities* (New York: Random House, 1964), esp. pp. 7–16. One of the most provocative treatments of the subject—and a blistering indictment of it as well—is Stillman and Pfaff, *Power and Impotence*, esp. pp. 167–182.

25. It is useful here to differentiate moralism and morality. As Cecil V. Crabb, Jr. has put it: "Morality has to do with the substance of behavior. It is conduct in accordance with a pre-determined code of behavior, and throughout Christendom this refers to behavior sanctioned by the Christian faith. Moralism (in the political sense) is concerned with appearance, with the concepts and language employed in foreign relations, with the symbols used, and with the way that ends and means are visualized and expressed publicly." See Crabb, *American Foreign Policy in the Nuclear Age* (New York: Harper & Row, 1960), p. 32.

26. Stanley Hoffmann, *Gulliver's Troubles or the Setting of American Foreign Policy* (New York: McGraw-Hill, 1968), p. 181. America's preoccupation with and seduction by the notion of harmony is very ably analyzed by Hoffmann, pp. 177–190—a perspective that is reflected in these pages.

27. Arnold Wolfers and Lawrence W. Martin, eds., *The Anglo-American Tradition in Foreign Affairs* (New Haven, Conn.: Yale University Press, 1956), pp. xv–xvi.

28. Stillman and Pfaff make this point in *Power and Impotence*, p. 125.

29. Walter Lippmann, "The Rivalry of Nations," *Atlantic Monthly* 181 (February, 1948), p. 18.

30. The literature on this period is extensive. Two of the more stimulating works are Loren Baritz, *City on the Hill: A History of Ideas and Myths in America* (New York: John Wiley & Sons, 1964); and Max Lerner's *America as a Civilization* (New York: Simon & Schuster, 1957), in which he elaborates a "theory of exceptionalism" as a kind of working hypothesis of an American character and culture that are distinct from others, especially Europe. See also Raymond Williams, *Culture and Society, 1780–1950* (Garden City, N.Y.: Anchor Books, 1960). For excerpts of the views of America's leaders in this context, see Wolfers and Martin, *The Anglo-American Tradition*.

31. Perry Miller, "From the Covenant to the Revival," in J. W. Smith and A. L. Jamison, eds, *The Shaping of American Religion* (New York: Basic Books, 1954), 1, p. 332. Miller argues that for Americans the exercise of liberty became the one true obedience to God.

32. In *Letters from an American Farmer,* Hector St. John Crèvecoeur wrote that the new society "is not composed, as in Europe of great lords who possess everything, and of a herd of people who have nothing. Here are not aristocratical families, no courts, no kings, no bishops, no ecclesiastical dominion, no invisible power. We have no princes, for whom we toil, starve, and bleed; we are the most perfect society now existing in the world." Everyman's Library edition (New York: E. P. Dutton, 1912), pp. 40–41.

33. Cited in Daniel J. Boorstin, *America and the Image of Europe* (New York: Meridian Books, 1960), p. 19.

34. Statements quoted in this passage are cited in Richard J. Barnet, *Roots of War: The Men and Institutions behind U. S. Foreign Policy* (New York: Atheneum, 1972), p. 19.

35. In 1927 Senator Hiram Johnson put it this way: "In all their long sordid international careers of blood and conquest these nations [Europe] have never done an idealistic, altruistic, or unselfish international deed." Quoted in Kirby Page, *National Defense* (New York: Macmillan, 1968), p. 196.

36. George Ball, "The Dangers of Nostalgia," *Department of State Bulletin* (April 12, 1965), p. 535.

37. The consequences of America's record of environmental transformation are ably presented by Hoffmann, *Gulliver's Troubles,* Chapter 5.

38. The writer is indebted to William Appleman Williams for the conception of "time" that is reflected in this section. See his *America Confronts a Revolutionary World* (New York: William Morrow, 1976), esp. pp. 38–40. It is also true that, from the beginning, some Americans accepted that condition as basically desirable and formulated a philosophy and a policy that much later came mistakenly to be known as isolationism. In this context, see Louis Hartz, *The Founding of New Societies* (New York: Harcourt, Brace, 1964), for the notion of a willed and self-conscious separation of America, divorced from its European background.

39. A seduction that continues to attract today. Witness Francis Fukyama's bold assertion in the wake of the Cold War's demise that we have reached the "end of history." See his "The End of History?" *National Interest* (Summer, 1989), pp. 21–40.

40. Williams, *America Confronts a Revolutionary World,* p. 20.

41. See Hoffmann, *Gulliver's Troubles,* Chapter 5

42. Tocqueville, *Democracy in America,* 2, p. 257.

43. Quoted in Kenneth W. Thompson, *Interpreters and Critics of the Cold War* (Washington, D.C.: University Press of America, 1978), p. xiv.

CHAPTER 2

Policy Imperatives: The American National Style

To do good is noble. To tell others to do good is also noble and a lot less trouble.

—Mark Twain

If national tradition represents the collective set of values that energize a people historically, national style reflects how those values are operationalized in the contexts in which the state must act. A nation-state will tend to act toward the world in a fashion that is never a carbon copy of any other nation-state. The concept, however, is not without its difficulties. Before we can proceed to address the question of style in American foreign policy, a number of these difficulties must be addressed.

First, like any premise or postulate, the notion of national style is useful insofar as it facilitates the creation of order for the analyst, but it shares with its subject matter the property of simplifying or distorting a much richer reality. It cannot be otherwise. The study of national style is not an exact science and therefore not yet productive of widely accepted generalizations. Nevertheless, it is possible, despite the lack of scientific rigor, to discover in most every nation common behavior features displayed by policy-makers and interested publics.

Second, it is well to remember that style is not substance. An American of the "left" and another of the "right" may disagree about every conceivable substantive issue, from the meaning of the American purpose to the causes of the "stagflation" of the 1980s, and yet they will couch their arguments and seek to persuade their listeners in ways that are similar to both and rather dissimilar to that, for example, of the German or the Italian. In other words, what is common to such distinctive historical figures as Theodore Roosevelt, Woodrow Wilson, Henry Luce, John Kennedy, George Meany, and David Rockefeller is not merely some of the values and prejudices one may find exhibited in their actions but also the terms in which they articulated their positions and couched their disagreements and the manner in which they acted upon them.

Third, the question of the uniqueness of a national style is one that should not be misconstrued. When one speaks, for example, of the "special nature" of America's national style, obviously, no single feature of that style is or can be wholly singular.[1] The uniqueness of a national style is not to be found in any one of its aspects but in the combination of features characteristic of each nation; what is unique is each nation's *experience*. Two nations with similar stylistic features will tend to react dissimilarly to their environments; being situated differently in the world, they will perceive their surroundings differently, and coming to the present situation with divergent historical traditions, their response to it will be molded by their domestic experiences and their "remembrances of things past."

Finally, as we shall be assessing the impact of America's style on its ability to maximize its national purpose, it should be clear that a nation's style can be both a source of strength and a manifestation of weakness—much like an individual's character. This is so, not simply because particular aspects are virtues and others are flaws, for the very same feature may be a factor for effectiveness or a reason for failure, depending on the nature of the problem or what is required at a particular time.

With an understanding of these realities, we can then posit that there does indeed exist a characteristic American national style of foreign policy—a habit of conduct in the world flowing from a distinctive belief system about what political action can and should accomplish abroad. In the pages that follow, we shall attempt to analyze some of the constituent elements of that style and, in the process, shall examine some special problems that arise from each or from a combination of them. One point is in order at the outset: The unsettling effects of the style with which America has tended to approach others in the world have from time to time been more disruptive than the substance of the world's problems themselves.

CONCEPTUALIZATION OF THE WORLD OF ACTION

Flowing from the storehouse of its historic traditions, America has developed over time a conceptualization or view of the world of action so as to give the fullest vent to the values of its people. The orientations characteristic of this viewpoint have provided the nation with an action framework by means of which it has sought to carry out its substantive goals and objectives. As such, these alignments have represented necessary conditioning factors in the translation of the values and beliefs of the country into the concrete initiatives of its foreign policy.

Suspicion of Outsiders

Americans have felt almost from the beginning that their ultimate salvation was to be found within their own country, and while recognizing that they must operate within the world as it is, they have argued they cannot trust themselves completely to it. Since Americans have had to participate in a world composed of people who, if not actually engaging in evil, were at least capable of it, their tradition tended to place a low appraisal on what they could accomplish in dealing with others. The benefits of foreign policy, as Charles Lerche has suggested, were thought to be by their very character limited in scope, and of only an inferior order of value. For what good America could obtain in the world, Americans have believed they must rely finally only on themselves.[2]

After its attainment of independence, of course, America had to deal with the outside world, whether it liked it or not, and for many years, that external universe was dominated by Europe. Distrust, even repudiation, of Europe was a leading theme in America's perception of the outside world. Europe stood for war, poverty, and exploitation; America for peace, opportunity, and democracy. There was also a profound sense of alienation from the various political forms associated with Europe's historical experience, most notably its reliance on balances of power. Indeed, throughout much of the nineteenth century and well into the twentieth, America, ignorant of the realities of European politics, inexperienced in dealing with the state actor participants involved, and highly critical of the morality of the European political process itself, remained deeply distrustful of its European colleagues.

This orientation was so strong that during America's involvement in the First World War, it insisted on retaining the role of "associated power" so as to avoid any undue contamination with the "sordid" politics of its erstwhile allies. Still later, the Roosevelt administration's suspicion of British motives during the Second World War contributed significantly to the inability of the country to deal intelligently with Soviet Russia during that conflict. Insofar as America's overriding goal during that conflict was the military defeat of Germany and the liberation of all the countries under its control, it chose not to address the legitimate security questions that Soviet Russia had been raising at the time. Obsessed with the fear that new spheres of influence in Eastern Europe would lead to another world war, Roosevelt and his advisers, in order to forestall this possibility, continually upheld the Atlantic Charter principles, sought to maintain a posture of non-involvement in the internal affairs of these states, and endeavored to postpone all political and territorial settlements until after the war. This, in combination with other American actions during the war, served to confuse and exasperate a highly suspicious and cynical Joseph Stalin and his associates. As a result, American policies unwittingly helped lay the foundation for the onset of the Cold War that followed.[3]

In retrospect, it seems that the major constituent element of the American distrust of the outside world has been the "European factor." It is in the specific character of the historic American relationship with Europe that one perceives the roots of the nation's propensity to have major reservations about its capacity to hold its own in a nasty, brutish world. Americans seem to have been unable to divest themselves entirely of the residues of their former colonial status. Out of that early period, and the revolutionary struggle with which it ended, emerged what might be called a chronic fear of American political inadequacy. Not so strong as to be labeled a sense of inferiority, and almost never verbalized, the feeling has nevertheless remained an important factor in America's approach to international relations.

Perception of Threat

Related to America's distrust of outsiders is the view that the world contains within it a real, palpable threat to the American way of life. Americans have proceeded from a set of assumptions whose imperatives dictated that the affairs of the world are to be understood in terms of a universal conflict of values—between harmony and disorder, freedom and tyranny, democracy and dictatorship. It has therefore been the belief of most of its people that, as the leading proponent of a system of equality in freedom, it is faced with an ever-present threat to its very being. While the balm of geography long conditioned this perception, the revolutions in transportation and communications of the nineteenth and twentieth centuries served to reduce dramatically the lead time to danger; as America grew in size and importance, this view took on added emphasis.

The nature and timing of America's relatively infrequent involvements in the European balance of power system before 1945 contributed to this perception. Whereas most great powers in the past have been major states during periods in which there were no long-standing friendships or hostilities, America's direct involvement in world affairs tended to occur in chaotic periods of major confrontation (1812, 1898, 1917, 1941, 1947–1950). Instead of alternations of restricted antagonism and constrained cooperation, characteristic of more moderate periods, America's involvement in European affairs has amounted to a succession of deep seated and intense enmities. This historical reality has left its mark on the national psyche.

The nation's involvement in both world wars dramatically intensified its conception of threat. Whereas for many years America lacked the capability to address the sources of this concern in any direct way, World War II put into the hands of the nation the means to do so. The sense of threat would certainly be one of the primary motivations compelling America, after 1945, to actively intervene in the world for its own security, for as the leader of the "free world," it was felt to be inevitable that America would be the ultimate objective of hostile attack.

In Defense of the Status Quo

One of the most persistent tendencies of America's traditional role in the world has been the desire to preserve and to defend what it has regarded as its own very special assets and accomplishments. As a nation that in its own eyes has seemed to accomplish more in terms of its aspirations than other peoples, this is certainly an understandable assumption to have made. Yet the implications of this posture for America's historic role in foreign affairs have been contradictory and burdensome for the nation.

"Status quoism" as a policy orientation has a reasonably precise meaning that derives from a nation's attitude toward the international situation as it understands it. A status quo state normally directs its policies at maintaining its relative position. Its strategy is a compendium of goals and objectives that are in a general sense defensive in concept and inspiration. Normally such nations are more preoccupied with improvising reactions to problems that originate from outside sources than with propounding positive long-range programs of their own. They typically entertain a major interest in peaceful international relationships, particularly in the functions of peaceful change. The primary substantive manifestation of status quoism is a sense of satiation, of fulfillment of the state's most basic aspirations.

The Sense of Satiation. Insofar as the basic concerns of any nation-state in the world are security and well-being, to the degree that Americans were successful after 1789 in their efforts to satisfy these goals, the evolving condition of America was revealed as one of intensifying satisfaction. In fact, the condition had reached the point where, after 1898, America would become more concerned with preserving its achievements rather than with supplementing them.[4] We had by this time " found it pleasant," in the words of George F. Kennan, "to picture the outside world . . . as similarly satisfied. . . . With everyone thus satisfied, the main problem of world peace, as it appeared to us, was plainly the arrangement of a suitable framework of contractual engagements in which this happy status quo, the final fruit of human progress, could be sealed and perpetuated."[5]

In the years after the Spanish-American War, there is little question that America reached virtual satiation. The country no longer had any burning territorial objectives; no major international adventures lurked on the horizon beckoning Americans forward. Left to themselves, Americans had no desire to harass vulnerable governments or to precipitate wars. They wanted only to be free to enjoy the fruits of their triumphs and, within reason, were quite prepared to allow others the same privilege. There was room for improvement, of course, but the nation was felt to be so well off that most of its leaders concluded that to pursue major altercations in an already enviable situation might imperil the basis of America's remarkable achievements. Indeed, the conduct of every administration since World War II has seemed to reflect the view that order and stability are the absolute lodestars of America's preferred international politics.

The Need for Order and Stability. Stemming in great measure from the fear of basic conflicts of ends in politics, and its resultant need for consensus, the American people have long had an ingrained dread of the deleterious consequences of any involvement in the Machiavellian power politics of other states. From the first days of the Republic, virtually all of its policy-makers endorsed a view of the international system as anarchic—potentially destructive of the nation's most important ideals. It was this view that would come to undergird the assumptions and operational style developed by the nation as it emerged in 1945 as a leading world state. Above all, it was a view that indicated that mankind's destructive impulses could be restrained only by a concentrated, long-term effort to impose an American-constructed sense of order on the world.

For America, order has meant the existence of peaceful and routinized methods of engaging in international politics, and stability the condition that accrues when these orderly procedures are so widely employed that nation-state behavior can be, in great measure, foretold. Together, these two notions represent the essence of the general approach to peace that has characterized American foreign policy in the years since World War II.[6] In this way, one sees America's identification with the status quo as most complete. Regarding the general area of international procedure, America insists that the mechanisms of international contact and adjustment must be peaceful and orderly. Peaceful progress—the mark of an orderly society—is the central ingredient of the status quo Americans have come in the twentieth century to perceive and to preserve in their own interest.

The Attitude Toward Change. It is sometimes assumed that a status quo orientation is one of merely preserving existing positions and of combating any and all change. This characterization is most emphatically not true of America. America has not so much been opposed to change, per se, as it has been leery of anything other than *peaceful* change. Indeed, in the classical sense, America began and has remained a nation driven by a profound fear of sudden, radical change. The kind of change expected by America is evolutionary progress, a continuation of a procession along the same sort of route that has proven to be salutary in its own history. Americans have come to see change essentially as the ever-expanding application of their own special principles and methods. It is a view of change that is quantitative, not qualitative. Within this concept of change there is an implicit vision—that of the future viewed most surely as the growth of what is best in the present. The model is already there, and all that is needed is that the reality become more and more like it—a world of self-determined, self-governing nations with nothing more than benign internal contentions and innocuous external disputes until the end of history.

The Status Quo in Action: America's Revolutionary
Revisionism

One of the distinguishing qualities of the American national style has been the revisionist implications inherent in the defensive posture that America has adopted toward most substantive questions in the twentieth century. This is especially the case since 1945. The kind of world in which Americans have wanted to live is one that cannot be achieved by merely holding on and permitting everyone else to look after themselves. The ultimate assurance of the American concept of the status quo requires action; America's leaders have long understood it cannot retain its relevance by withholding help to others or by avoiding necessary action to advance the conditions leading to peace. The national purpose of America, then, has frequently demanded not treading water or immobility but basic change in many sectors of the globe. But the nature of that change—indeed, the very content of the "revolutionary message" therein that the nation has symbolized—is one that is often overlooked or misconstrued by observers of the American scene.

It has often been said that Americans are the truly genuine revolutionaries of the modern era. In the nation's relationship to the rest of the world the assumed message has been thought to be crystal clear: It is revolution that America has been given to "export," and it is its democracy that has represented the substance of that revolution. Alas, like many other components of the American self-image, the reality has not matched the assumption. The tradition of America has been so qualitatively different from that of other states that both its democracy and the nature of its revolutionary experience raise serious questions as to the meaning of these assertions.

The Political Content. Since our society has on the whole been a relatively affluent one, and was fairly democratic to begin with,[7] the term *democracy* for America has tended to have a predominantly political meaning. In other societies where fundamental social change is required, democracy is not necessarily a political concept alone but is most significantly a social ideal as well. The foundations of America's liberal culture of democracy were laid by the Puritan migration of the seventeenth century, rather than by social revolution, and this fact has made it difficult for many people in this country to understand the movement of social revolution abroad.[8] It is only in the twentieth century that this problem has become entangled with the nation's destiny. As a world power for the first time, this reality would bring the American people onto a plane, face to face with an experience of revolution that on the domestic level they have not had.

There are both formal and substantive issues involved in the effort of a nation, created out of migration, to understand the experience of social revolution. In the case of social upheaval, the grounding of the nation in the Puritan escape from Europe produced from the outset major problems of appreciation. For one thing, the process of migration made possible a remarkable degree of ease and success for the achievement of democracy in America, since the old feudal enemies were left behind in Europe and it was therefore unnecessary to liquidate them. Moreover, America's unique abundance conditioned the manner in which democracy developed in this country. Most importantly, that abundance set it free of the need to remedy any feudal inequities that might have developed in the new world, therefore stripping it of the necessity for the violent sort of social revolution that other countries have undergone. It is in the nature of this twofold experience where one must seek the *raison d'être* for America's response to revolution elsewhere. This is why Americans have difficulty understanding not only the violence of French-style revolutions but the fact that, from America's vantage point, they always seem to "fail."

Thus, as America did not arise out of a revolutionary experience but rather out of migration experience, the very process of escape, of getting away, was America's substitute for the European psychology of social revolution. In viewing that psychology, it projected our ancestors not only out of Europe but across the entire American continent also. In this way, the legend of the covered wagon would come to supplement the myth of the Mayflower. It is in this sense that the American Revolution may be most usefully viewed as a nationalist upheaval, not a social one, for it did not involve a sweeping, all-encompassing reconstitution of the values and institutions of the society. To be sure, there was a "radical aspect" to that upheaval, but there was no extremism as that term has been understood elsewhere.[9] This is why the American people have had an almost instantaneous sympathy with revolutionary movements abroad, but only *in terms of nationalism,* because these are terms with which we can identify within our own "revolutionary experience."

Then, too, one must remember that as America has in its historical experience come to identify with the values of liberty, freedom, equality, self-determination, and the dignity of the individual, it has done so not at the expense of the harmony and consensus that has represented the essence of its being. Perhaps this is the main reason why Americans have had difficulties in exporting their democracy, for they do not understand or appreciate very well the social roots of other peoples' developmental traumas. We are afraid that "things will get out of hand."

Yet to the degree that the basic values of America have demanded great transformations in many parts of the world, the nation has consistently violated the stereotype of the status quo state in its role as a modern great power. On this point, America is truly a revisionist nation. In this way, for example, one can better understand the historic commitment of its leaders to the removal of the conditions on the planet that breed war. For America, a stable world order must contain procedures that will make change possible, feasible, and acceptable, all the while limiting state action to something short of overt violence. America's participation in the First World War, personified at the time in Wilson's own *weltanschauung,* puts this historic inclination in clear perspective: "We are glad

. . . to fight thus for the ultimate peace of the world and for the liberation of its peoples . . . for the rights of nations great and small and the privilege of men everywhere to choose their way of life and of obedience. The world must be made safe for democracy. Its peace must be planted upon the tested foundations of political liberty."[10]

In assuming this posture, however, there has existed an elemental ambiguity, tension, paradox, and ultimately, a profound contradiction in America's approach to the world. In an international arena of revolutionary social upheavals, Americans like to remind themselves and others that their country was once the "first new nation," the product of a "revolution" that was the initial step in the long process of colonial emancipation—the first clarion call of the coming golden age of universal equality in freedom. At the same time, as America reminds others that it stands for the dignity of the individual, it also refers to emphasize orderly (e.g., constitutional) procedures, the preeminence of legality, avoidance of violent, disruptive conflict—in short, most everything that seems to be incompatible with the revolutionary forces of change in the world today. The consequences of this dualism in America's outlook have led the nation into a variety of situations, of which Vietnam proved to be the most traumatic, that have resulted in compromises of its national purpose of equality in freedom.

The Materialist Component. There is another aspect of America's status quoism that has been historically revisionist, even stridently so, and that is the sense in which America's bourgeois economic culture has been "permanently revolutionary." What we are talking about here is the revolutionary implication of that ongoing marriage between the nation's economic abundance and its own dynamic internal energies. Americans have proven themselves capable of destroying entire landscapes and then of reconstructing them, of tearing down cities and of creating new ones, on a scale more vast than that of any other people in the world. This is the drive that has nourished the immensity of its industrial achievement. When the American people's more positive Puritan intensities have been permitted utterly free reign, unrestrained by any sort of feudalist residue, this is when one discovers the great dynamo qualities of its tradition most in evidence. It is this revisionist aspect of the materialist component of the American tradition that has exerted such an electrifying impact upon other nations. The consequences for action flowing from that reality have been monumental.

For one thing, Americans have been exceptionally prone to regard all things as resulting from the unfettered choice of free will. Probably no people have had so little determinism in their philosophy. As individuals, Americans have tended to regard all their achievements in life as things of their own making. The distinctive system of voluntaristic relationships characteristic of American life may be seen in this light.

Second, the competitive spirit of the American people is in large measure a response to the environmental largesse of the nation, and to its ample potentialities for exploitation. In this way, the American character may be viewed as a group of responses to an unusually competitive situation engendered by that environment. Whatever the materialist content of much of this competition, it has generated a drive for accomplishment within the American psyche that has had great impact abroad.

Third, as America's frontier long demanded innovation and imagination in order to be overcome, there was little room there for social pretense. The typical American came to measure his own worth by the distance that he progressed from his point of departure rather than by the position that he occupied at the moment. Class hierarchy, when it was considered at all, was conceived as a ladder whose rungs were to be ascended rather than as a set of pigeonholes into which one was to be thrust permanently. Mobility and change came to be regarded as the natural by-products of the typical American's quest for success, and departure from the patterns of the past viewed as a matter of course. The possibilities of both horizontal mobility (across cultural lines) and vertical mobility (upward movement through class hierarchies) held out by the American experience have been demonstrated over and over again. The implications of the challenge to traditional notions of authority and status inherent in this reality have represented one of America's most profound revolutionary revisionist impacts upon the world.

Finally, for the first time in the history of man, human beings have been led to believe that there is something better in life than mere subsistence. The "revolution of rising expectations" engendered, at least in part, by the American experience has been thought of as at last freeing the status system of its one great historic blemish—a condemnation of the vast majority of men and women to lives of want. The universe of action for America has come to mean, by inference if not by choice, a world of movement, of upheaval, of "progress." It is therefore a universe that contains a crucial intellectual issue, for it involves an implicit contradiction of the prevailing notions of "consensus," balance," "order," and "moderation" in this country.

It is ironic that while the great majority of the nations of the world now covet America's great material accomplishments, some having even succeeded in emulating the habits of action that have seemingly been so responsible for them, perhaps the greatest problem facing America today is how to relate its material standard of living, with all its social consequences, to the processes of rapid change and development in the world. America's revisionist posture has served to unsettle a host of other social systems—cultures that have functioned for hundreds of years with few great social dislocations but that, partly as a consequence of increasing contact with America, have more often than not developed immoderation, disorder, dissension, and a release of mass passions to the detriment of this nation's long-standing commitments to order, consensus and harmony.

THE UNIVERSALIZATION OF VALUES: AMERICA'S MISSIONARY ZEAL

While all cultures tend to view themselves as distinctive in some respect, others seem to be possessed of a felt need to promote and revere their differences. And a significant few, among whom number America, have been so confident of the value of their peculiarities that they have been active missionaries to a larger congregation.[11]

Deeply implanted in the American self-image is the belief that this nation typifies the aspirations and desires of the whole world; that in the management of its own internal affairs America has conducted a living laboratory experiment directly relevant to the hopes and fears of other peoples. Common to most sectors of American society has been the view that America's history—particularly the successes of its political democracy, its material prosperity, and its achievement in damping down social discord—provides a prototypical solution for the world's disorders. Possessed of an economy productive beyond what any people has ever known, a standard of living still the envy of many, and a democratic political constitutional framework that is already the oldest in the world, Americans have long been persuaded of the general validity of their institutions. It is a conviction that rational argumentation and periodic failure have not been able to shake in the years of America's leading world role.

As with its sense of uniqueness, the sources of America's propensity to universalize its values may be seen very early in its history. On the eve of the American Revolution, Thomas Paine wrote in *Common Sense* that "the cause of America is in a great measure the cause of all mankind. We have it in our power to begin the world again."[12] In these utterances, America's foremost revolutionary publicist aptly typified the belief that the "self-evident truths" of the Declaration of Independence should be extended to unfortunate peoples wherever they might be. This concept of the universality of America's intrinsic truths, of its mission to the outer world in their name, was succinctly conveyed by the motto engraved upon the Great Seal of America—*novus ordo seclorum*, "a new order of the ages."[13] Almost a century later, Lincoln observed that the Declaration of Independence gave "liberty, not alone to the people of this country, but hope for the world for all future time. It was that which gave promise that in due time the weights should be lifted from the shoulders of all men."[14] These statements summed up what most Americans came ultimately to believe: that their "new order" would have a profound impact upon the substance of global affairs and upon the evolution of mankind.

The themes of self-determination, uniqueness, and isolation in time were integrated in the universalist rationale of Manifest Destiny and given flesh during the Spanish-American War. That struggle became something more than a war; it was turned into a crusade. It was America's destiny, said William McKinley, to bring the benefits of a civilized world to backward peoples.

The moralist content of the growing universalist pretentiousness of America's foreign policy was clearly reflected in the attitude of Theodore Roosevelt. His "Peace of Righteousness" represents the quintessence of the universalist stimulus in American diplomatic history. The first Roosevelt believed that wars to discipline uncivilized peoples were justified. The self-appointed policemen of the world to ensure a peace of righteousness were to be the civilized states with military strength, led by America.[15]

Under Woodrow Wilson a view of the world as a great stage on which Americans could choreograph an inspiring design for peace, progress, and prosperity came to predominate. A key to Wilson's views in this regard were summed up in his belief that America was the only idealistic nation in the world. Wilson believed that America's historic mission was to create an international society where liberal, democratic, and capitalist values of order, law, and harmony would prevail.[16]

This outlook was reflected in Franklin Roosevelt's Four Freedoms message to the Congress in January, 1941.[17] To the extent that statements like the Four Freedoms represented serious enunciations of American foreign policy goals, they epitomized the historic American belief that an organic connection exists between the extension of democracy and the maintenance of global peace and stability. Implicit in these notions is an American way of thinking about the world that amounts to an apprehension of it as ripe for reform—a rationalization of the American experience. "The idols Americans worship," Max Lerner pointed out, "are . . . the idols of their own culture transposed upon the world scene,"[18] the progeny of America's early beliefs and historical experience.

AMERICA'S LEGALISM

Legalism refers to America's foreign affairs tradition that international behavior, both that of our own and that of others, should be in consonance with established legal norms. It is the belief that it should be possible to control the chaotic and dangerous behavior of states in the international realm by means of legal rules and restraints. Because of a tradition highly influenced by a commitment to consensus and harmony in their political and social affairs, America's leaders attach to the legal (formal) side of international relations far more importance than do those of most other nations.

From the first days of the Republic, Americans exhibited a taste for the utilization of legal principles both to defend and to justify their foreign policies. This belief has flowed in part from a natural inclination to extend the Anglo-Saxon concept of common law into the international field and to make it as germane to foreign governments as it is relevant to individual Americans. It also stems in some measure from the legacy of America's own development—from the recollection that Americans were able, by their own ingenuity, to reduce to relatively harmless dimensions the conflicts of interest among their original inhabitants. Change—the proper sort of change—has to come through, and be guaranteed by, legal provisions, not merely by means of the political process.

The Historical Record Reconsidered

For Americans, insofar as a "world of law" has been the preferred state of affairs, the country has been an innovator in the development of rules of international law so as to encompass more and more of the interactions of states. Historically, this impulse has taken two forms, one being the elaboration of new legal principles to formalize evolving international relationships that have reached or are reaching stability,[19] and the other the development of rules of law embodying nation-state obligations in an effort to align the actual conduct of states with certain humanitarian values.[20] Viewed analytically, America's performance in this context has been one of both great accomplishment in terms of furthering its national purpose and, at times, bitter, frustrating failure. On more than one occasion America has permitted its tradition of consensus in politics (the instinct for harmony) to get in the way of rational and productive decision-making.

Shortly after the emergence of America as a constitutional democracy in 1789, one begins to see the acceptance and espousal of international law as a means of defending the young nation's vulnerability within the international realm.[21] This was a natural and logical policy orientation for a relatively weak country to take, most especially when one remembers the strategic international situation in which the fledging nation found itself. As a small state, America appealed to international law to protect its trade with belligerents and to restrain its own citizens from undertaking aggressive acts (usually on behalf of democratic principles) against other states. Later in the nineteenth century, it began to develop a more positive view of international law. Rather than emphasizing law merely as a shield, the American state now sought to use legal principles as instruments for solving difficult political issues by means of mediation, arbitration, and adjudication.[22] In some areas of state behavior, legal norms were not developed or lacked specific application to the problems at hand. On these occasions, America interpreted the "rules" of international law to conform to its own interests, such as its post-1865 self-proclaimed "right" to intervene in Latin American countries in order to collect public debts and to generally provide for order. As such, this represented an attempt to tailor international law to justify America's new, expanded interpretation of the Monroe Doctrine.

Reliance on international law became by the end of the nineteenth century a dominant characteristic of American foreign policy, but as America took on great state status in the world arena of the twentieth century, the emphasis on legalism shifted to what may be called the "rule of law" approach. As a small state, its legalism had concentrated on the preservation of neutral rights and duties and, later, on arbitration of differences. Now, after 1898, we see a rapidly increasing propensity by America's decision-makers to frame their world view in a more vague and sweeping manner. The relative specificity that characterized its previous conduct dissipated into generalizations that amounted at times to insignificance and/or arrogance.[23]

A number of explanations may be offered to account for this development, best seen as a function of the specific situation in which America found itself after the First World War. First, the nation studiously avoided participation in the most readily available source of a potentially more realistic and generally acceptable foundation for international law—the League of Nations. Instead of involving itself directly in that "futile" attempt to stage-manage what it regarded as the unsavory Machiavellian intrigues of the international system, America instead chose, for its own peculiar parochial reasons, to march to its own tune.[24] Second, since there was little agreement during the interwar period upon the basis for an international legal order, high sounding phrases about the rule of law allowed the major powers, including America, to maintain a symbolism of legality while the crass "law" of the jungle actually prevailed.

More broadly, this desire for an all-encompassing system of law, which would define the duties and obligations of all nations, reflected certain fundamental factors of the parochial American experience: an ongoing success of legal and organizational remedies for problems in America's own history; the intellectual appeal of "formalized" solutions for short cutting politics, especially "power politics"; the great impact upon Americans of a deep belief in material progress; a view that sees in economic terms man slowly but inevitably improving his lot and, in political affairs, moving toward a universal constitutionalism and peace. For America "the road to heaven" must be an orderly and peaceful one. Only by means of an inexorably rational, logical, incremental, and temperate train of progress could man come, in the end, to live in equality in freedom.

The fruits of this sort of thinking came to full flower in America's foreign policy formulations during the first four decades of the twentieth century—epitomized in the transformation of America's "recognition" policy under President Wilson, in the efforts to deal with the problem of war during the Coolidge and Hoover administrations, and in the theory and practice of "Stimsonianism."

It was under Wilson's guidance that major changes were brought off in America's historic recognition policy. Previously, America (along with nearly all other governments) had followed the practice of recognizing a new regime as the *de facto* (existing) government of a country, irrespective of its political ideology, if it demonstrated the capacity to act—that is to say, if it could exercise authority over its own territory and discharge its international responsibilities in a reasonable manner. Wilson replaced this long-accepted and most sensible recognition test with a new criterion: "constitutional legitimacy."

According to the new principle, *America* would do the evaluating and then decide whether a particular government had the "support of the people" and whether it acted in their "best interests." A related Wilsonian principle was an attempt to differentiate between an incumbent government that America opposed (for whatever reason) and the people, whose interests America, naturally, was trying to promote.[25]

The propensity to employ the recognition mechanism both as a means to avoid having to deal with unpleasant realities and as a device to punish those with whom America is in disagreement has remained an integral part of the nation's foreign policy posture down to the present day. It is a policy preference that would be utilized on many occasions after 1945 as America took up the burdens of "Cold War" against Soviet Russia and the forces of a seemingly implacable and ever resourceful "international communism."

Another area in which America's peculiar historical partiality for legalism reared its head at this time was the question of warfare. Indeed, the American conception of war itself was a product of the reliance on consensus, its related preference for order and stability, and fear of violent change that underlay its general approach toward the world. This partiality was particularly evident in America's attempts after World War I to arrive at multilateral arrangements for disarmament, especially among the great European powers. The most direct American involvement in this effort was in the field of naval armaments, but it also took an active part in the comprehensive disarmament discussions that were carried on in Geneva under the auspices of the League of Nations during the decade from 1925 to 1935. Herculean energies were expended on these discussions. The record of the deliberations runs into something like 30,000 pages contained in some 500 documents, all of which was presented in the form of a report to the Disarmament Conference. While all this was going on, of course, the new realities already gathering momentum in Weimar Germany would soon sweep away this labor from the stage of world history as though it had never existed.

Then there were the complex and protracted attempts to delineate a definition of aggression. Both under the League of Nations and, later, the United Nations Organization, international law commissions were created for the purpose of developing a rational, comprehensive, and universally acceptable definition of aggression. Thousands of hours were devoted to this task by some of the best brains in the world. The assumption that went into these efforts was the view that the concept of aggression in fact lent itself to such efforts. It was a sterile exercise undertaken by men of goodwill in good faith. Then, as now, it was simply not possible in a world of nation-state sovereignties to consummate such an undertaking successfully. In the present age the inability of the United Nations effectively to address itself always everywhere to "acts of aggression" on the international stage must be seen, in part, to be a reflection of this conceptual failure.

As the specialists who squandered their intellectual resources seeking a precise delineation of aggression discovered, the notion of "aggression" has meaning only when there is an unambiguous, forcible violation by a foreign state of the territorial frontier of a widely recognized state in which a government has established law and order. But the very notion of aggression makes sense only in a situation where it is possible to differentiate peace and war. Furthermore, it is more applicable in an international relations context that is generally stable. Its usefulness is problematical in an age of revolutionary upheaval where the very subject matter of international law is in dispute. Is it any wonder that many of the rules of international law dealing with war and civil strife have been in a state of flux for much of the last half of the twentieth century?[26]

A bizarre illustration of the legalist tradition in American foreign policy was the 1928 Kellogg-Briand Pact, the so-called Pact of Paris, negotiated by the French and American foreign secretaries and designed to put an end "once and for all" to the problem of war. Surely this was one of the most ill-conceived episodes of modern history. Here was an instance in which competing groups of well-meaning peace enthusiasts in America and in France succeeded in goading their respective governments to try to negotiate the termination of war. The effort that went into that negotiation was formidable. People were encouraged to place great hopes and expectations in the enterprise. Millions were caught up in the seriousness of it all. Despite all of this, the final result could not have been more disappointing.[27]

But perhaps the most characteristic manifestation of America's fondness for generalizing a rule of law approach was the Stimson Doctrine of Non-Recognition. Stimsonianism was a logical extension of Wilson's earlier transformation of America's historic recognition policy. It was President Hoover's Secretary of State, Henry Stimson, who first prominently articulated the notion that if aggression were permitted to go unpunished in one place, this by infection would lead to a general destruction of the system of world order. Thus, he argued, what America should and must do in those instances was not to "recognize" the results of such aggressive acts. It was this policy that was first applied in 1932 to the Japanese conquest of China's northeastern province, Manchuria, and later to Italy's aggressions in North Africa. The results were predictable. In neither instance were the aggressors persuaded to abandon their "selfish national interests" for the sake of world order.[28]

In retrospect, one has to say in all fairness that America's rule of law approach to international affairs may well have helped prepare the way for the outbreak of the Second World War. By contributing to the dictators' cynical disregard for the other countries' willingness to fight, it emboldened them in their increasingly provocative efforts at domination. Only with this awareness in mind can one truly understand the profound sense of disillusionment that gripped many young people during and after the war.[29] So, too, the "realist" reaction to these events that came to dominate America's foreign policy after 1945 was in great measure a deliberate repudiation of America's historic legalism.

And, yet, despite the denigration with which it was viewed after the war, the legalist orientation would not go away. As America moved into the post-1945 era of Cold War, the legalist mode would be reasserted in the context of the hegemonic conceptualization of alliance that characterized the nation's attempts to forge more secure relationships in response to the perceived Russian threat. It would also be evident in the long effort to reach an arms control understanding with Moscow and its attitude toward the many problems associated with colonial emancipation and socioeconomic development in the Third World.

Legalism Recapitulated: A Balance Sheet

The historical inclination of America to put great stress on legal approaches in its dealings with other nations has been a mixed bag at best. In the first place, the American conception of law has been something rather different from mainstream thinking in this area. In reaction to their aversion to the sticky intricacies of international bargaining—with their inherent dangers and potential for disaster—Americans substituted early on a quite distinctive framework of law: a system, it was believed, that must rest upon agreed principles and that required, if it was to work, an administrative and policing mechanism by which that framework could be impartially enforced upon all.

The appealing logic of this approach was that it extended to the international system the achievement that has made the internal life of America itself so successful. The superficial assumption it makes is that there is in fact a consensus among nations on a sufficient number of principles to make law observance possible—that most, for example, oppose war and aggression; indeed, that all are prepared to accept the same definition of aggression. Implicit in these notions are deeper assumptions about the universality of the democratic impulse, the self-evident character of principles of social justice, and the general validity of the values of individualism, consensus politics, and public altruism that have long been hallowed in America's own unique experience.

George Kennan, in a most cogent critique of this American legalist position, put it this way:

The mind of American statesmanship, stemming as it does in so large a part from the legal profession in our country, gropes with unfailing persistence for some institutional framework. Behind all this, of course, lies the American assumption that the things for which other peoples in this world are apt to contend are for the most part neither creditable nor important and might justly be expected to take second place behind the desirability of an orderly world, untroubled by international violence. To the American mind, it is implausible that people should have positive aspirations, and ones that they regard as legitimate, more important to them than the peacefulness and orderliness of international life. From this standpoint, it is not apparent why other people should not join us in accepting the rules of the game in international politics.[30]

Why, indeed? Yet the record of concurrence by others in these rules is spotty, to say the least. As we have pointed out, America's domestic success in achieving whatever sort of consensus on law and government it has developed reflects as much the lucky fact of its historic geographical advantage and great abundance as it does the fact that this country was founded as a free act of organization and legal compact. It was this most fortunate environmental context that facilitated the development of America's own special native brand of politics—a democratic theory that was deeply grounded in the Enlightenment faith and belief in the viability of reasonable action to improve things in life.

One suspects that a major reason for America's cultural myopia here is that its policy-makers have frequently confused the realities of municipal law within their own country with their hopes for international law, thereby imposing upon the latter, and upon the substance of international politics, additional burdens.[31] Viewed historically, if the problem was the existence of war, it was merely necessary to outlaw it; if the peril was aggression, a precise legal formula defining and proscribing it was the goal, and a refusal to recognize its fruits a proper concomitant; if states trembled in fits of insecurity, reassure them with security pacts heaped upon one another; if a state threatened the peace, pass appropriate resolutions. Despite the goodwill underlying such approaches, they have, on balance, accomplished rather less than hoped for in the years of America's involvement in the world; in fact, they have frequently weakened the conduct of its foreign policy, for alliances, declarations, and legal formulas at odds with the realities of international political life tend to urge on the lawless reckless adventures, and upon the law-abiding a whole chain of emotional responses, beginning with that most debilitating of attributes—self-righteousness.

Role of Force. Nowhere has this legalist conception of reality had greater impact than on America's thinking about the role of force in international politics. It was in this sense that William James once described America's reliance on international law as a "moral equivalent for war." Perhaps the single greatest difficulty that America has had in handling the vast national power it has accumulated in its short history has been how to integrate and operationalize in an intelligent, rational, and humane way the use of force in its foreign relations.

The great difficulties that have tended to plague American thinking on the problem of force have had deep roots in the legalist condition of the historical American mind. The tendency to assume that force can be dealt with in the isolated compartments of disarmament conventions or arbitration treaties, divorced from the harsh realities of power in the outside world or from viable strategic doctrines evolved to meet mutual interests and needs is a case in point. America's decision-makers continue to wrestle with the dilemma of how to employ force effectively and productively in its relations with other nations. The Vietnam War was particularly troublesome in this regard. That they have not yet discovered a working formula to that end testifies, at least in part, to the straitjacket that its legalist tradition continues to impose upon its mental outlook.

A second major difficulty in America's legalist posture has been the almost inevitable association of these legalist ideas with moralistic ones: the carrying over into the affairs of nation-states of the concepts of right and wrong, the assumption that nation-state conduct is a proper subject for moral judgment. The linkage ensues because those who assert there is a law tend to be outraged by the lawbreaker and feel a moral superiority over him. For "moralistic" persons, it is a source of great personal gratification to condemn those who believe that politics primarily concerns interests. Such people are, in their eyes, instigators of the disastrous doctrines of power politics and thus block the road to a peaceful and harmonious world order. Replace these people and surely international cooperation will supplant the ancient rivalries and conflicts of political man; a system of law will inevitably replace the existing quasi-anarchy that habitually characterizes the power-ridden international order.

And when the indignation of the moralist spills over into military conflict, satisfaction is usually not obtained until the lawbreaker is reduced to total submissiveness.[32]   A war that is fought in the name of high moral principle seldom ends before a total domination or destruction is realized. Total war and total victory are two of the high prices that we have come to pay in the twentieth century for this heavy reliance on the legalistic-moralistic approach, for the view that war's object is unambiguous victory distorts the truth that war's end typically involves either the achievement or non-achievement of certain specific objectives.

Third, in America's relationships with other states, its simple belief that all nations are basically like itself ignores the tremendous variation among countries some of whose borders are largely accidents of history, poorly related to economic realities, and therefore, often in a state of upheaval. Changes in their status are more readily accommodated by diplomacy, not "law," which tends to be too abstract, too inflexible, too hard to adjust to the demands of the unpredictable and the unexpected. Nor has the tendency of America to differentiate among the inhabitants of other nations been of much help either. America's fondness for making legal distinctions between governments whose views it disapproves and the people that these regimes presumably represent are distinctions that few foreign peoples have grasped or appreciated and, to the degree they are reflected in particular policy initiatives, not productive of cordial relationships between America and the countries involved.

Finally, the tendency of American elites to invoke abstract legal principles to justify their policies, and to place undue reliance upon legal concepts as substitutes for enlightened strategy, has tended to produce rigidities in the nation's foreign policy that have often limited the nation's facility in making effective policy and in choosing among appropriate means for the carrying-out of that policy. The result is that courses of action, once taken, are difficult to change and, even when modified, have to be presented so as to fit somehow into the accepted legal mold. This would be especially true of its alliance policy after 1945 and more generally a persistent element in its relationship with Soviet Russia in these years.

AMERICANISM: A CRUSADING NATIONALIST IDEOLOGY

"America," Arnold Toynbee once wrote, "is not just a place but an idea, producing a particular kind of society. When immigrants choose to become Americans they are expected to accept the political values of this society, associated with the egalitarian and democratic traditions of the American Revolution. As an immigrant country, perhaps only Israel is comparable in the demands it makes for the acceptance of an ideology as well as a territorial nationality."[33]

The peculiar style of American nationalism owes much to the Puritan Ethic's concept of a universal set of values applicable for all Americans. When the English Puritan came to America, he was in a sense no longer completely "English," which meant that he had to find a new national identity. And where was that identity to come from if not from Puritanism itself, the ideal part of which he had extracted from the English whole and which he alone possessed? Over time the part became, as it were, a new whole, and Puritanism itself blossomed into "Americanism." A crisis of self-definition implicit in the migration experience resolved itself in a new nationalist ideology compounded out of the migrant value-structure.

A major factor in the development of this nationalist ideology was that basic strain of puritanical moralism that has long existed in the American mind—a moralism that has impelled Americans to conceptualize a world of fundamental right arrayed against implacable wrong. In such a world view, there can be no question of the ultimate victory of the truth. In this sense, the extent to which the concept of Americanism has become a compulsive ideology rather than simply a nationalist term may be more easily understood.[34]

America's ideology has amounted more to an allegiance to definitive values, to a pervasive creed, rather than to a mere national consciousness. More than any other democratic country, America has tended to make ideological conformity one of the conditions for good citizenship. A national myth of separateness, exclusivity, and superiority was integral to America's national formation and development. It is those qualities of the historical American mind, along with its sense of mission, and the ever present characteristic overweening moralism, that serve most clearly to differentiate America. All the elements of a powerful ideological creed are present: a sense of mission, historical necessity, and evangelical fervor. America thus emerges in some sense as the most ideological of the great powers in the last half of the twentieth century.[35]

Every ideology has universal aspirations in order to rationalize and justify its acceptance among human beings. The self-image is clear. America seeks no colonies or territorial annexations. It opposes colonial empires.

America, after all, did not set out at any time in its history, as did the Nazis, to dominate the world. There was no cold, cunning calculus behind America's interventionism after 1945, we are told, in contrast to that of Soviet Russia's. According to the self-image, until America came onto the scene, never before in history has a nation sought to play a major role in the world with any aim other than that of domination; America consequently finds itself in an unprecedented position in the annals of man. In this degree, it is believed, America is one of the very few nations whose ideology transcends the national interest of the country, for America's nationalism is not one designed primarily to further special American ambitions or interests, even if its success has had that result. It goes far beyond the narrow universe of nation-state interactions to encapsulate the very best about man and society.

It is this self-image, of course, that frustrates and angers so many of those who have had intercourse with this country. But to charge, as some do, that the ideology that came after World War II to undergird America's role in the world was nothing more than a hypocritical exercise is to miss the point. The nationalist ideology of America can only be understood by taking the official rationale for its conduct at face value. America's fundamentalist belief system rests on a theory of law-giving that ultimately imparts to its component values a kind of driving, restless energy. According to many of its most representative spokespersons, the goal of American foreign policy has always been to create, or at least to facilitate, a peaceful world increasingly subject to the rule of law. But it is America that must "organize the peace." America imposes the "international interest" by laying down the ground rules for the affairs of people everywhere. America towers above the international system, not within it. First among equals, it stands ready and anxious to be the bearer of the law.

Thus, America's involvement in world politics has for many years tended to be one of mobilizing public opinion by means of this exalted, if operationally ambiguous, ideology.[36] This was the case prior to its entry into World War I when President Wilson conceptualized the American intervention as a "rescue operation" to "save the world for democracy." It is also true with respect to the nation's involvement in the Second World War, for it was the Atlantic Charter, with its insistence upon the Four Freedoms, that became the Roosevelt administration's rallying cry for the conduct of the country throughout that long and bitter conflict.

And when America, after 1945, came in the fullness of time to commit itself to a policy of opposition and confrontation with the forces of "Godless communism," it did so not merely in terms of specific security concerns, or even with a clear understanding of the nature of the "threat" that was confronting the nation, but rather in terms of an "unselfish" commitment to "save the world." Once again, the manner in which America conducted itself would generate considerable confusion and trauma both for itself and for the "beneficiaries" of its actions—the rest of mankind. For in the years after assuming the mantle of a self-imposed world leadership, America's ideology would draw its people to do what could not be done, to interpret reality in terms of illusion, and more ominously, to justify its actions in terms of their "higher" meaning. In such a world as this, the emperor would be badly in need of a set of clothes.

NOTES

1. To take two different examples, historians have long noted that the so-called paranoid style in politics is evident not only in the history of America but in the evolution of Russian culture, in the politics of the French Right, and in a variety of non Western cultures as well. See in this regard, Richard Hofstadter, *The Paranoid Style in American Politics and Other Essays* (New York: Alfred A. Knopf, 1965); and Philip Williams, *Crisis and Compromise* (Hamden, Conn.: Archon Books, 1964). Consider also the shared pool of values in British and American history stemming from a common experience of non-involvement in the quarrels of continental Europe. See here again Arnold Wolfers and Lawrence W. Martin, *The Anglo-American Tradition in Foreign Affairs* (New Haven, Conn.: Yale University Press, 1956).

2. Charles O. Lerche, Jr., *Foreign Policy of the American People,* 3rd ed. (Englewood Cliffs, N.J.: Prentice-Hall, 1967), pp. 107–108.

3. For this view, the author is indebted to a number of groundbreaking and insightful works, although he may not necessarily agree with all of their viewpoints and/or conclusions. Among the more important of these writings are: Lynn Etheridge Davis, *The Cold War Begins: Soviet-American Conflict over Eastern Europe* (Princeton: Princeton University Press, 1974); Voytech Mastny, *Russia's Road to the Cold War: Diplomacy, Warfare and the Politics of Communism, 1941–1945* (New York: Columbia University Press, 1979); Martin F. Herz, *Beginnings of the Cold War* (New York: McGraw-Hill, 1966); Albert Resis, "The Stalin-Churchill Secret 'Percentages' Agreement on the Balkans, Moscow, October, 1944," *American Historical Review* (April, 1978), pp. 368–387; Hugh B. Hammett, "America's Non-Policy in Eastern Europe and the Origins of the Cold War," *Survey* (Autumn, 1973), pp. 144–162; Walter LaFeber, *America, Russia and the Cold War,* 5th ed., (New York: Alfred A. Knopf, 1985); Diane Shaver Clemens, *Yalta* (New York: Oxford University Press, 1970); Robert Garson, "The Atlantic Alliance, Eastern Europe and the Origins of the Cold War," in H. C. Allen and Roger Thompson, eds., *Contrast and Connection: Bicentennial Essays in Anglo-American History* (New York: Macmillan, 1976), pp. 296–320; and William Taubman, *Stalin's American Policy: From Entente to Detente to Cold War* (New York: Norton, 1982).

There is, of course, considerable disagreement in regard to just what motivated the American government during this period. The critical literature centering on the Second World War era regarding the origins of the Cold War is extensive. Several groups of analysts emerged over time arguing one or another point of view. This writer falls within the so-called post revisionist school of thought—a perspective that accepts the main contention of the revisionists that America must bear a heavy share of the responsibility for the onset and intensification of the Cold War but that denies that it was deliberately created by its policy-makers for either political or economic reasons.

4. It is true, of course, that during much of the nineteenth century the country had a dynamic expansive foreign policy that was an accurate reflection of a rather evident desire to flesh out its "natural frontiers." Until America achieved

continental security, hemispheric preeminence and economic maturity, it had long-standing revisionist impulses that undergirded its policies.

5. George F. Kennan, *Realities of American Foreign Policy* (Princeton, N.J.: Princeton University Press, 1954), p. 16.

6. For a discussion of these concepts, see Lerche, *The Foreign Policy of the American People,* p. 134.

7. There was already a tradition in colonial America that, in terms of modernity and utilitarianism, was even more advanced than that of much of Europe. For one thing, there was neither a well-developed aristocracy nor a pronounced peasantry on the American land that corresponded to the European prototypes. The revolutionary spirit of social democracy had been developing in America since the seventeenth century, during which time there was a continual sloughing off of some of the medieval "marginalia" that clung to it as it migrated across the Atlantic. See in this regard Robert A. Goldwin, ed., *Left, Right and Center: Essays on Liberalism and Conservatism in the United States* (Chicago: Rand McNally, 1967).

8. On this point, see Louis Hartz, *The Liberal Tradition in America: An Interpretation of American Political Thought since the Revolution* (New York: Harcourt, Brace and World, 1955).

9. American society was already spiritually and socially democratic when the "radicals" created their famous state constitutions in 1776. The American colonists had been prepared by prior experience for the responsibilities imposed upon them by their new institutions. It is certainly a matter of relevance that the American leaders were men like Sam Adams and Patrick Henry who had sat in colonial assemblies for years rather than a group of alienated Latin American creoles whose experience had been confined to the fringe aspects of government and administration.

10. Cited in Albert Shaw, ed., *President Wilson's State Papers and Addresses* (New York: George A. Doran Co., 1918), pp. 380–81.

11. As Edward Burns has noted, in *The American Idea of Mission. Concepts of National Purpose* (Westport, Conn.: Greenwood Press, 1957), p. 5: "[T]o a greater extent than most other people, Americans have conceived of their nation as ordained in some extraordinary way to accomplish great things in the world." Ralph Gabriel regards the idea of the mission of America as one of the three basic themes in America's democratic philosophy. See his *The Course of American Democratic Thought Since 1815* (New York: Ronald Press Co., 1940).

12. Thomas Paine, *Common Sense* (1776), Nelson F. Adkins, ed., (Indianapolis, Ind.: Bobbs-Merrill, 1953), p. 19.

13. It was Jefferson, no less, who suggested that the official insignia of the new nation depict the Children of Israel being led ever forward by a shaft of light from the heavens.

14. Lincoln's views, interestingly, are cited in John Foster Dulles, *War or Peace* (New York: Macmillan, 1950), p. 254.

15. Virility was the necessary ingredient to lead the world, according to Roosevelt. Peace would result from an aggressive and fearless policy pursued by a just people. There are occasions, he wrote in 1905, when war is preferable to peace because a "just war is in the long run far better for a nation's soul than the most prosperous peace obtained by acquiescence in wrong and injustice." Quoted in Harry Magdoff, *The Age of Imperialism: The Economics of United States Foreign Policy* (New York: Monthly Review Press, 1969), p. 45.

16. Although hackneyed by much quotation, Wilson's speech on the Fourteen Points merits one more repetition because of its eloquent evocation of the idea of the American mission: "We entered this war because violations of right had occurred which touched us to the quick and made the life of our own people impossible unless they were corrected and the world secured once and for all against their recurrence. . . . The program of the world's peace, therefore, is our program." *Congressional Record,* 56 (January 8, 1918), p. 691.

17. In which he outlined the task for America was to make the world secure for the existence of four essential human freedoms: for free speech and expression, for religious worship, and from want and fear. The text may be found in Senate Foreign Relations Committee, *A Decade of American Foreign Policy: Basic Documents, 1941–49,* 81st Cong. 1st session (Washington, D.C.: Government Printing Office, 1950), p. 1.

18. Max Lerner, *America as a Civilization* (New York: Simon & Schuster, 1957), p. 920.

19. One twentieth-century example is the question of international civil aviation. See the International Air Services Transport Agreement, drawn up at the Chicago Conference on Air Transport in 1944. *Proceedings of the International Civil Aviation Conference* (Washington, D. C.: Department of State, 1948–1949).

20. Perhaps the best-known post-1945 example of this is the 1948 United Nations Convention on Human Rights, a document in whose drafting America played a leading role.

21. See, for example, Alfred Leroy Burt, *The United States, Great Britain and British North America from the Revolution to the Establishment of Peace after The War of 1812* (New York: Russell and Russell, 1961); and Bradford Perkins, *Prologue to War: England and the United States, 1805–1812* (Berkeley: University of California Press, 1961). For the intellectual background, consult Felix Gilbert, *To the Farewell Address: Ideas of Early American Foreign Policy* (Princeton, N.J.: Princeton University Press, 1961).

22. A cogent illustration is the conflict between this country and Britain that grew out of the American Civil War. The gist of the dispute centered on a series of British "interventions" in the American conflict, most especially the building and arming of Confederate fighting ships in British ports. After some wrangling, the dispute was submitted to arbitration, resulting in the 1871 Treaty of Washington, which disposed of the claims to the mutual satisfaction of both parties.

23. In all candor, it should be pointed out that there long tended to be a curious dichotomy in America's dealings with others in terms of its propensity to invoke the canons of international law. Its invocation of these "rules" has tended, on balance, to be more reflective of its relationships with stronger powers and not so much the case when dealing with weaker nations.

24. The League should have been in a position to generate legal norms for the maintenance of international society, but it did not, in part because of its "empty chairs." Never at any time during the history of that body were all the major states of the international system members at the same time. On the American approach at this time, see Selig Adler, *The Uncertain Giant: 1921–1941, American Foreign Policy between the Wars* (New York: Macmillan, 1965).

25. This discussion of Wilson's recognition policy relies in part upon Howard F. Cline, *The United States and Mexico,* rev. ed. (Cambridge, Mass.: Harvard

University Press, 1963), pp. 553–562. See also the author's unpublished monograph, "The Estrada Doctrine and Recognition in International Law," for a discussion of the historical American tendency to politicize recognition.

26. See Richard Falk, "Janus Tormented," in James Rosenau, ed., *International Aspects of Civil Strife* (Princeton, N.J.: Princeton University Press, 1971), pp. 185–248. See also his monumental compendium of articles in *The Vietnam War and International Law* (Princeton, N.J.: Princeton University Press, 1969), esp. Vol. 2.

27. For an account of this episode, see Louis E. Ellis, *Frank B. Kellogg and American Foreign Relations, 1925–1929* (New Brunswick, N.J.: Rutgers University Press, 1961).

28. The Stimson Doctrine not only predictably failed to deter future Japanese aggression in Asia but may have facilitated and encouraged further expansion by Japan and other Axis Powers by implying that in a crisis America would do nothing of a provocative nature to defend its avowed foreign policy principles or diplomatic interests. See George F. Kennan, *American Diplomacy, 1900–1950* (New York: Mentor Books, 1952), esp. pp. 41–56, for a trenchant criticism of America's earlier behavior with regard to the Open Door Policy. For an account of the Stimson Doctrine, see Robert H. Ferrell, *American Diplomacy in the Great Depression: Hoover-Stimson Foreign Policy, 1929–1933* (New Haven, Conn.: Yale University Press, 1957).

29. It is not often appreciated in this country that the great enthusiasm with which thousands of young men and women turned to "socialism" in both Eastern and Western Europe during and after World War II was in some sense attributable to their feelings of disgust and alienation from the dominant prewar "bourgeois" politics in their own countries. At the very least, the failures of their political leaders to prevent the war, if not their outright complicity in its onset, fueled this reaction; so, too, the general failure, especially in Eastern Europe, of many of these regimes to respond to the very real social and economic grievances of their peoples. All of this facilitated the appeal of Soviet Russia in the immediate postwar period and, no doubt, contributed to the relative ease with which the Russians were able to ingratiate themselves into these areas.

30. Kennan, *American Diplomacy,* pp. 83–84.

31. The attractions of government service for lawyers has long been a fact of life. Several studies have shown that, in the years since 1945, a rather high percentage of government appointees to important foreign policy positions have had legal backgrounds. A number of disconcerting questions have been derived from these studies: To the degree that lawyers are trained never to discuss their clients' cases out of court, how has this affected the willingness of governmental officials to dissent publicly from the nation's foreign policies when they are in fundamental disagreement with them? And if they do criticize in the public forum, to what degree are their careers in jeopardy? Robert McNamara's refusal for many years to publicly air his apparent departure from American policy in Vietnam is a case in point. See, in this regard, John Franklin Campbell, *The Foreign Affairs Fudge Factory* (New York: Bobbs-Merrill, 1972).

32. Franklin Roosevelt's insistence upon the objective of "unconditional surrender" during the Second World War may be seen in this light. On the relationship between law and force in American history, see Edwin C. Hoy, *Law and*

Force in American Foreign Policy (Lanham: University Press of America, 1985).

33. Arnold Toynbee, *America and the World Revolution* (London: Oxford University Press, 1962), pp. 29–30.

34. The concept of ideology is employed in these pages to mean a relatively coherent, systematic set of beliefs about man's place in nature, in society, and in history that elicits the commitment of significant numbers of people to (or against) sociopolitical change. These beliefs have a certain integrated, unified quality; they "hang together" with a consistency that, while it may be artificial or illogical, is at least recognized as a general standard for imposing constraints on belief elements. It also generates emotions that serve to tie people together and contains a vital action component; that is to say, it consists of habits of action shared by many human beings who act in concert or who are influenced to act together in order to accomplish posited ends. Defined in this way, ideology does not exclude a set of ideas essentially concerned with merely a class or a nation if it relates the place and needs of that section of humanity to the place of man in general. The matter of ideology, of course, has been pursued and commented upon by many writers. On this question, see George Lichtheim, *The Concept of Ideology and Other Essays* (New York: Random House, 1967); Max Lerner, *Ideas Are Weapons: The History and Uses of Ideas* (New York: Viking, 1939); John Plamenatz, *Ideology* (New York: Praeger, 1970); and Karl Mannheim, *Ideology and Utopia* (New York: Harcourt, Brace & World, 1955). On ideology in the American context, see Michael H. Hunt, *Ideology and U. S. Foreign Policy* (New Haven, Conn.: Yale University Press, 1987).

35. Even more so than Soviet Russia, which, under Stalin, rapidly lost its ideological fervor and élan.

36. Bruce M. Russett and Elizabeth C. Hanson, *Interest and Ideology: The Foreign Policy Beliefs of American Businessmen* (San Francisco: W.H. Freeman and Co., 1975), argue that the closer people are to the "levers of power," the more beliefs concerning foreign policy issues merge into a structured ideology. A number of studies have suggested that interrelatedness of attitudes is closely associated with information level and with political interest. They conclude that "Those who have a sizable amount of accurate information and a high degree of interest will relate various facts and principles to produce a coherent set of beliefs" (p. 141). See, also Norman Nie, "Mass Belief Systems Revisited: Political Change and Attitude Structure," *Journal of Politics* 36, No. 3 (August, 1974), pp. 540–591; and Frederick D. Herzon, "Intensity of Opinion and the Organization of Political Attitudes," *Western Political Quarterly* 28, No. 1 (March, 1975), pp. 72–84.

CHAPTER 3

The Approach to Problem-Solving

It is better to fail than to succeed in doing harm.

—Simone Weil

How Americans deal with problems stems from the attitudes concerning human affairs that they have come to possess. This conception is part of a national experience whose relevance to the outside world is uncertain, because the conditions in which it has taken root have been so different from conditions anywhere else. Out of that experience Americans have elaborated a distinct manner of approach to the difficulties they encounter—a multifaceted style of response that constitutes a unique cultural way of comprehending the world instrumentally. The specific answers to particular problems have changed from period to period, but the general approach has remained the same—a mode that is almost guaranteed to raise more questions than it answers.[1]

THE EMOTIONALLY VOLATILE AMERICAN

Emotion is a highly visible element in this nation's attitudes toward the world. Among the earth's major states, perhaps only the Russians compare with Americans in both their fondness and capability for indulging their emotions and prejudices on the international stage. The public typically follows the course prescribed by their current likes and dislikes. This tends to promote in American public opinion a peculiar "wavelike" quality manifested in wide emotional swings of the pendulum from one extreme to another. The emotional volatility of Americans is most noteworthy in their frequent impatience in the face of persisting obstacles and in their preference for dichotomies as a point of departure in relating to these problems.[2]

Americans expect to accomplish more than most; their national experience has seemingly demonstrated it. And as their culture historically has emphasized direct social action with speedy results, they tend to prefer quick solutions to problems, with no excuses accepted for delay. When the answers are not always soon forthcoming, impatience takes over, causing Americans to chafe under the necessarily tedious and delicate course that diplomacy normally requires. This leads occasionally to the advocacy of showdown or all-out techniques when less extreme measures might be more appropriate.

The preference for framing problems in terms of dichotomies in America's mental makeup has been another characteristic evident in its emotional makeup. Throughout our history there has frequently been expressed the notion that the only acceptable outcomes of a situation are the extreme ones. How often have public attitudes in America thought in terms of total war or total peace? This dichotomous formulation of problems grows out of the notions of impatience and emotionalism and in turn influences each of them. The combination of impatience and the framing of problems in terms of dichotomies makes Americans more vulnerable in several respects when applied to foreign affairs in which progress is often tortuous and painfully slow. Consequently, this cultural trait can operate to intensify the conflicts in which the nation finds itself.

It encourages Americans, for example, to underestimate the tenacity of problems and to think in rather ambitious terms. It leads them to the brink of temptation to take on a larger role than they (or anyone else) may be able to fill. It makes continued crisis difficult to endure, eroding national self-control and perspective. It generates tremendous pressures for action that officials often find very difficult to withstand. And it exposes the nation to frustration when intractable problems remain unsolved.

REASONING BY ANALOGY

To a certain extent, conceptual lag is inherent in the human condition. There seems to be a natural predisposition for people to look at their current situation in terms of events that preceded it, imparting to those earlier triumphs and tragedies lessons that must automatically apply to the contemporary context. But no two sets of events are ever exactly alike, and any nation that permits itself to be unduly influenced by the attractions of analogous reasoning in its foreign policy-making is going to be in for considerable difficulty.

Reasoning by analogy singles out, in two complex events being compared, aspects that are common to both and urges that since they were essential in the first case, they must be decisive in the second. America's policy-makers have been plagued by an inclination to think by analogy—a habit that is aggravated in our own case by the presence in government of many lawyers who are prone to reason by reference to precedents. An undisciplined utilization of analogy in policy analysis poses a number of dilemmas for those who engage in it.

First, reliance on analogous reasoning leads to a mode of thought in which one situation is referred to in terms of another, and disembodied plans lead to policies with little grip on reality. Such an orientation often leads to an inability to see new events for what they are; instead, there is an attraction for reducing them to something reassuringly familiar. Thus, resort to analogy may be an escape from instead of an instrument of analysis, symptomatic of a habit of employing history to suit one's own purposes.[3] In America's case, its decision-makers have evinced a persistent fondness for using history as a kind of grabbag from which they extract lessons to prove their points. The performance of America's decision-makers in the years after 1945 is a case in point. Perhaps the best illustration of this fallacy was the frequent American habit after 1945 to look at the world, threatened as it was felt to be by an "international communist conspiracy," in terms of the Western response in 1938 to Hitler at Munich. The difficulty is that when Americans invoke Munich in order to exorcise appeasement anywhere, they forget that Munich itself was the product of disastrous decision-making by analogy. The British prime minister, Neville Chamberlain, insisted upon making an analogy between the pre–World War I balance of power involving essentially moderate states and the European states of the 1930s. As he soon discovered, Hitler and Bismarck had even less in common than what was believed.

Second, an added consequence of this tendency in foreign policy is a kind of volatility. The urge to analyze issues in terms of analogies instead of tackling them on their merits encourages a commitment to policies long after they have outlived their usefulness, and then a rather abrupt dismissal of them once their counterproductiveness has become obvious, at which point they are replaced with new dogmas that often have the same effect. Hence, the frequent alternation of rigidity and sudden about-faces that one sees sometimes manifested in American foreign policy formation over the years.

UNILATERALISM

One of the earliest behavior patterns that emerged in American foreign policy was unilateralism—an inclination toward independent action in dealing with the issues of international relations. From the beginning the nation has sought to maintain the widest possible latitude in its decision-making. The American unilateralist approach to problem-solving is rooted in the colonial experience of the nation, watered by its first encounters with European diplomacy. In the international affairs of the eighteenth century, the American colonists often found themselves deeply immersed in conflicts, the causes and purposes of which they seldom understood or appreciated. For many Americans, these conflicts were fought for goals and objectives embedded in British foreign policy and, therefore, not in the best interests of the North American colonies.[4]

The experiences of the Revolutionary War reinforced the American inclination for avoiding what they viewed as the incessant intrigues of European politics. Americans were greatly impressed (depressed may be a better word) by the deviousness of European diplomacy during that struggle. Receiving a crash program of education in the sophisticated diplomatic practices carried on by their allies, Spain and France, the American revolutionaries quickly learned that their "friends" supported the anti-British undertaking largely in terms of their own interests, rather than for love of any such concepts as "equality," "freedom," or democracy."[5]

After obtaining victory in the Revolutionary War, the new nation saw no reason to change its attitude on these matters. Distrust of Europe's traditional diplomacy early surfaced as a persistent suspicion of the balance of power concept. The idea of promoting an equilibrium among nation-states pursuing their ends at the expense of one another was a natural concomitant of the endemic turmoil and disruption of the French Revolution and Napoleonic periods. In retrospect, there is little question that the successful pursuit of that balance was responsible for generating a century of relative peace, from the Congress of Vienna (1815) to the outbreak of World War I (1914).[6] But America's leaders rejected the balance of power device as an instrument for maintaining stability in the international system; rather, they viewed it as a grievous structural defect, a primary cause of conflict. Their unilateralist posture was viewed as an appropriate response to this situation. It was a view that, in one form or another, has persisted to the present day and one that has been displayed in a wide variety of situational contexts.

The War of 1812 can be seen, at least in part, as a result of the American predilection for unilateralism in its foreign policy. The American propensity for going it alone, in addition to a lack of sophistication of the country's leaders, led to a series of foreign policy mistakes culminating in that unnecessary conflict. The young nation's unwillingness to bargain with its British and French adversaries certainly facilitated the drift into the war situation that occurred.[7] America's unilateralist stance in this instance was not defensible in the national interest. In their disputes with the British, Jefferson and Madison insisted on a sweeping settlement that would have had their enemies in London renounce their "illegal" behavior on the high seas. All along, America could have achieved a workable arrangement that would have smoothed over relations for a while by removing questions of international law, and even morality, from the bargaining table. Such was not to be the case.[8]

The Monroe Doctrine epitomized the evolving diplomatic pattern of unilateralism underlying the nation's determination to walk its own path in world affairs without the assistance of anyone else. Although the Doctrine certainly clarified the American desire to maintain absolute independence of judgment in its foreign relations, the country lacked the necessary capability to translate the Doctrine into policy in the field. It remained for the British navy to implement the Doctrine in the American nation's best interest.

Later in the century, as America's capability increased, it was able to give fuller vent to its unilateralist inclinations. This became especially evident in Latin America. In 1879, for example, Ferdinand de Lesseps, the builder of the Suez Canal, negotiated a deal with Colombia to excavate a waterway across the isthmus of Central America. Secretary of State William Evarts let the French government know that America regarded the project as an unfriendly act, and the French suspended their plans. The British also occasionally ran aground on American unilateralism in the area. One such incident was a dispute concerning the boundary line between Venezuela and British Guiana, which led finally in 1895 to Secretary of State Richard Olney accusing the British of violating the Monroe Doctrine. The matter ended in arbitration.

It is during the First World War where one finds the American inclination toward unilateralism in its international conduct most striking. When the nation finally became aroused sufficiently in the spring of 1917 to join in the conflict, it fought alongside Britain, France, and Russia but refused to be allied to them. Thus, the term often appearing in the histories of that war to describe this relationship is "allied and associated powers." As an "associated" but not an "allied" power, even in war, the American people sought to maintain their pristine independence of outlook.[9]

One also sees unilateralism as an integral part of America's isolationist stance during the twenty-year period after World War I. According to Paul Seabury, isolationism signified America's "preference for autonomous action in world politics and a disinclination to be bound by alliances or by any supranational agreements committing the nation in advance to policies which might involve the use of force in war."[10] This was certainly true in regard to its Latin American policies during these years. The nation freely interpreted the Monroe Doctrine, first in the direction of more overt intervention under the impetus of the Roosevelt Corollary and "dollar diplomacy," then later in the opposite direction with the Good Neighbor Policy.

And when, in 1941, the nation would be forced by events to involve itself actively in the Second World War, America felt itself almost required to act unilaterally, irrespective of what the country's particular response to Axis aggression might be. Hampered by its traditions from using its military, economic, and even its moral influence abroad in concert with other nations, it would pay a fearful price for its failure during the Second World War years to cooperate more meaningfully with its new-found allies. The full dimensions of the dilemma inherent in this historic tendency in America's international conduct would become most apparent after 1945. For the ensuing five decades, the unilateralist posture would represent an enduring and highly controversial theme in this nation's foreign policy, most especially in its conception of alliance.

AMERICAN UTOPIANISM

The element of idealism or utopianism has been one of the most highly visible components of this nation's problem-solving style. Like so many of their traits, the utopianism of Americans has been both an asset and a handicap in their relationships with others. In a positive sense, it has been apparent in the great optimism and confidence exhibited by Americans in the face of obstacles. More troublesomely, it may be seen in the view that victory will inevitably result from the application and replication of one's labors. It is also evident, in a negative sense, in the historic tendency of Americans to downplay long-range thinking in their planning. In terms of all these characteristics, utopianism remains one of the more persistent and wide-ranging components of the American national style.

Almost every observer of the American scene from the birth of the nation to the present day has pictured Americans as an optimistic, exuberant, and versatile people determined and able to solve problems that have harassed mankind from the beginning of history. Optimism and confidence welled up from the objective situation in which the American people found themselves—qualities that represented a source of early greatness for America. It was the faith and expectations of America's restless peoples, nurtured by an unshakable belief in the potentiality of the future, that helped them overcome the pain and deprivation of the westward drive into the rough and unknown reaches of a land that surely flowed with milk and honey.

These qualities of mind played a major role in America's subsequent accomplishments, especially the drive to industrialize that preoccupied the nation in its adolescence. America's confidence fed, and was in turn reinforced by, the success with which its people obtained the many material benefits that have come to mark their twentieth century existence. Their optimism facilitated achievement, and their achievement generated further confidence in what could really be done. Consequently, one of the most striking aspects of the American approach to problems is a strong emphasis on the ability to make progress and to resolve whatever difficulties that loom up along the way. It is ironic therefore that this very strength of character has proven to be a source of problems in the nation's foreign relations, for the awareness of the perpetual renewal of the American success story contributed much to the view that America's future existence on earth was destined to be marked by victory.

America's Development in Historical Perspective

It is well to remember that the degree to which Americans came to think in this fashion was at least in part a result of the manner in which the nation's own important internal problems arose. The comparatively widely spaced sequence in which their environmental challenges occurred not only facilitated the relative ease with which the nation was able to deal with them but colored its perception of the nature of problem-solving itself. Unlike many countries before and since, America has always had sufficient time to confront and reduce to manageable proportions the manifold, complex difficulties associated with modernization as an integral part of the developmental process.

Modernization may be most usefully seen as a fourfold historical revolutionary challenge confronting any people in its national development, the constituent elements of which we may label state-building, nation-building, participation-building, and welfare-building. In other words, the crucial questions confronting newly independent states have always been:

How are the territorial boundaries of the state to be decided in terms of effective government control—that is, at the same time, capable of being recognized as legitimate by others?

How is the nation to be formed out of a variety of indigenous ethnic groups who may not speak the same language, profess the same religion, possess the same cultural backgrounds, or even share common values?

How are illiterate and unskilled peasants and villagers to be given the right to vote before they even know how to read and write or even understand what government is?

How are the goods and services of the modern era to be distributed to such people in a relatively fair and impartial manner?

In a word, the typical new country faces an authority revolution, a national revolution, a participatory revolution, and a welfare revolution at one and the same time. One of the hard realities of the modern age is that most newly independent countries have had to confront these revolutionary challenges simultaneously; indeed, the leaderships of these new nations often do not even have a choice as to which mix of these challenges they may want to respond. Invariably, they must give priority to state- and nation-building before they can begin to respond to demands for participation and welfare.

In America's case, it had a luxury of time to deal incrementally with these revolutionary challenges. By the beginning of the nineteenth century the Founding Fathers had largely settled its national problem by successfully integrating most of its inhabitants into the spirit and ethos of a vigorous ideological nationalism. By the middle of that century, the country's territorial peripheries were essentially determined—an accomplishment that served the happy function of siphoning off the excess creative (and destructive) energies of its people. These two potentially destructive issues were largely resolved before the questions of participation and welfare became so pressing so as to overwhelm the nation's capacity to respond. It is only in the later nineteenth and early twentieth centuries that the matter of a more equitable distribution of goods and services to all its citizens begin to exert great pressure. And the demands by women, black Americans, and other minorities for equal access in the political and social processes of the nation has only been a major issue in the present century.

Even so, America had to endure a monumentally destructive civil war in order to finally consummate the consensus. This fact is often forgotten today by those who assume the existence of ultimate and stable harmony in America—a happy blend of liberal and conservative ingredients. The blunt truth is that in terms of its domestic politics, the American reality has yet to correspond wholly to the self-image. And when these assumptions have been projected onto the world stage, major problems have ensued.

Foreign Policy Implications

Statesmen who view international politics as a permanent test of wills tend to incur reprobation. After all, this is not a view that corresponds to the dominant American conception of conflict, but since a failure of events to satisfy anticipations is the normal condition in life, Americans, who expect so much more than what the world can provide, tend to criticize the world rather than their presumptions. In particular, "a people that has never experienced defeat" will be more prone to consider even the possibility of defeat as a disaster than will peoples who are more conditioned to cycles of success and failure in their historical experiences. More generally, America's relative domestic success in problem-solving has tended to promote a smug complacency about history. That complacency has assumed many forms over the years. Failure in the American lexicon is the non-solution of problems. Indeed, the idea of failure in America has verged on the treasonable. Because the American self-image has been one of enormous success in the handling of our domestic affairs, when we have entered the international arena we have assumed that with sufficient effort and goodwill on all sides, the problems of humankind can be harmonized with a minimum of difficulty. Americans have long been appalled at the "terrible sloppiness" of international politics. They view themselves as a nation of neat technicians whose capacity for action is the ultimate antidote to the world's travails.

It should thus not be surprising to discover that the popular attitude toward foreign policy, once America has actively engaged itself in international affairs, has usually been an urge to "set things right," "to get the job done," "to move it forward." Americans disapprove of purposeless action; they have typically sought affirmative goals of improvement, of rectification, of reorganization. Moreover, the "right" answers have often been conceptualized as ones that will forever resolve the difficulties, removing the problems to the category of the "not-to-be-thought-about-again." Not only have single issues been addressed in terms of locating their own appropriate solutions, but also the long-range mission has been viewed as a world structured into a single, self-adjusting mechanism. This, Americans believe, is the most fruitful approach in eliminating for all time the scourges of violent death and destruction.[11]

Thus, history is viewed as a continuum in which the "pilgrims of progress" move inexorably forward rather than as a mountain range in the midst of which one encounters innumerable obstacles. Foreign policy is seen not as a fluid interplay of multitudinous divisive forces or as a congeries of conflicts and crises but as an activity designed to avert and deter the occasional problems that might slow down the march. No wonder that the requirements of thinking for the long range have rarely had a great attraction for Americans. The successful improvisation style of the American nation has not required it.

The Denigration of Contemplation

"Men who live in democratic communities," Tocqueville wrote, "not only seldom indulge in meditation . . . they naturally entertain very little respect for it. A democratic state of society and democratic institutions keep the greater part of men in constant activity; and the habits of mind that are suited to an active life are not always suited to a contemplative one."[12] Americans have seemed to be especially prone to avoid engaging in a systematic plumbing of the inner motivations of human behavior. The predominant view appears to be that if we are fortunate—which, of course, the nation has been throughout much of its history—we can somehow muddle through with the support of our extraordinary economic wealth and technological capability.

An understanding of this trait tells us a great deal about the appeal for Americans of open-ended, universalist approaches to reality. Such approaches have generally been uncritically accepted. From generation to generation, pronouncements of foreign policy have assumed the character of holy writ, but they are dogmas of style, of approaches to reality (e. g., to its problems) rather than of content—principles of action rather than fixed attractions to ideological stars. While it is true that the poles around which the America problem-solving style have operated are ones that entail some kind of long-range commitment, it is commitment not in terms of careful planning for the future but as a perpetuation of those problem-solving traditions that have been most congenial in its past. The most persistent and the most hallowed of these imperatives has been that of America's pragmatism.

AMERICA'S PRAGMATISM

When Abraham Lincoln spoke of the "dogmas of the quiet past [being] inadequate to the stormy present," he was not calling for America to reject that past but to reach deep down into its reservoir of experience to deal with its latest problems. That statement was in the finest tradition of America—squarely within the mainstream of the nation's own "philosophy" of history. In fact, it should come as no great shock that America's disdain of reflective thought would provide the background for one of the few original contributions of this country to the field of philosophy—the very field in which such contemplative processes are held in the highest esteem. America's major "gift" to the philosophical tradition has been the doctrine of pragmatism—the notion that any idea that generates practical results is useful and therefore "true," provided that it does not disagree with or contradict experience. The essence of pragmatism resides in its repudiation of the idea of ultimate or metaphysical truth and in its notion that through the application of scientific knowledge truth should be sought after, not as an end in itself but as a means for improving human existence.

From the perspective of this philosophical tradition, the proper standards upon which to base human action must be "experience," "concreteness," and "immediacy," rather than the traditional ethical or moral values long associated with religious teachings or monolithic social and political ideologies of one sort or another.[13]   What better approach to rationalizing the American experience than to judge truth to be ultimately one of representing the quintessence of that experience! In this sense, pragmatism reflects and universalizes not only a certain "deification" of methodology in America's national style but also the nation's self-image of uniqueness and its sense of isolation in time as well.

The Pragmatic Method

Of one thing there can be little doubt: Americans are an "achieving people" par excellence. "Ours is a how-to-do-it society," Kenneth Keniston has written, "and not a what-to-do society."[14]   The nation's whole history may be seen as a kind of glorification of a way of acting, a pattern of behavior resting on a set of assumptions that correspond to the American experience, and not so much as a mode of thought.

It is America's vaunted pragmatism that has been felt to be primarily responsible for the great achievements of its people. Seen in retrospect, the American frontiersman's practical bent of mind has often been held up as one of the most crucial factors responsible for the taming of the West. Since the closing of the frontier the pragmatic method has been adjudged to have been successfully translated into ever-new areas: from the overcoming of great obstacles in the construction of the nation's far-flung transportation systems to the assembly-line production of its food; from the country's awesome achievements in science, medicine, and communications to its landing of men on the moon. All bear eloquent testimony to the great appeal and "self evident truths" of this tradition: We are bigger and better; ingenuity, improvisation, and practical application make all the difference; the machine is power and magic.

It should also be abundantly clear by now that certain liabilities have pertained in respect to the pragmatic approach. That same confident, energetic, improvising style becomes—by means of its neglect of the long term—frustrated and impotent when confronted with intractable or persisting problems.[15]   No where has this reality been more clearly demonstrated than in the country's foreign policies.

In the first place, America's pragmatic style has often left the impression that its people possess an absolute competence to do anything. Issues that the leaders of other countries may regard as insoluble, and that they may prefer to leave to the healing resources of time to resolve, are seen as America's business. The great optimism that has worked wonders at home energizes Americans in other lands, yet the inability of these finely honed instruments to accomplish in other countries what they achieved at home leads Americans once again into frustration. Moreover, preoccupation with the pragmatic approach too often precludes or overwhelms the long-range vision that is required for a wiser utilization of these instruments or for an understanding that they cannot or should not be employed.

Second, America's brand of pragmatism ignores the long range and middle ground in human affairs. Rather, the pragmatic approach means all too frequently emphasis upon the urgent as proposed to the important. Circumstances, not people, seem to prioritize the nation's issues. A manner of determining policy that is preoccupied with means, and that assumes that ends are ordained by the nation's traditions, or dictated largely by context, imparts to America's view of problems a sense of shortsighted obtuseness. In the country's wartime experiences, for example, the need to win has detracted from the importance of shaping the postwar situation in which it has found itself. Decisions made for purely military reasons, on the grounds of immediacy, tend to adversely impact the political conditions with which the nation has subsequently had to live. A pragmatism that concentrates on such short-term emergencies is more remedial than preventive—a palliative at best.

Finally, in America's case, the pragmatic approach, which demands the most economical resolution of problems as they occur by methods sanctified by the nation's successes, complicates the ability of the country to cooperate with others who do not share in the American consensus and who conceive of the world in a different fashion. Because, to cite one instance, America's own historical experience of successful environmental transformation has led its people to be enthusiastically optimistic in their conception of problem-solving, we should not presume that other peoples in the world necessarily share these views. If we can comprehend this point, there is likely to be less disappointment and frustration with the responses of others. But such understanding is difficult for Americans. It is at these moments when America resorts to the preaching and lecturing manner that is so demeaning and infuriating to other people. "Moral pretensions and political parochialism," Reinhold Niebuhr commented, "are the two weaknesses of the life of a messianic nation."[16] The marriage of pragmatism and moralism in America's international conduct has been a most provocative relationship indeed. This is particularly true in our insistence upon viewing the problems we face as crises.

The Ubiquity of Crisis

America's understanding of crisis owes much to the pragmatic spirit of its people, betraying as it does the highly parochial experience of its successful modernization efforts. It is not any wonder that the nation's need for harmony, nurtured in the contexts of its historic distrust of power and its uncertainties concerning outsiders, would have produced in its collective life a compulsion to view problems as a series of crises, each to be contended with as best it could according to the vagaries of the moment. America's propensity to view its problems as crises reflects both an acute psychological disposition and an instrumental bias that has come to be a substitute for enlightened strategy.

A belief in universal crisis would come to mark much of twentieth century American foreign policy. It is a belief that derived not only from the ideological propensities of these years but from the most sentimental and self-indulgent traits of the American intellectual and political tradition. The habit of Americans to label their problems as crises can only be understood in the framework of a historical inclination of a people that has conceived of themselves as unique among nations, whose own conduct at home is seen to have been blessed by Providence, and who have taken upon themselves the task of spreading the "message" of their achievement to the rest of humankind. Implicit in this formulation is the desire to escape from the crisis (not of our own making) by first resolving it and then withdrawing from it. The motivation is clear: Only by dealing decisively with its crises can America finally retreat from the foreign policy arena altogether and settle down to the one thing that is most important to it—the people's internal business.

But the ubiquity of problems viewed as crisis, pressing ever in on the consciousness of America's decision-makers, does not permit such utopian conduct. The vicissitudes of history require that there be some sort of planning after all in the nation's approach to problems. Consequently, there *has* been a continuity of sorts that one finds in the fabric of America's policy-making, but it is continuity that exists in terms of contingency planning for crises. It is almost as if we do not feel there is very much to be gained from any systematic, long-range handling of problem situations.

Thus, the American "strategic style" is one that has come to be predicated essentially on the confrontation and resolution of crises—a habit of action that conceptualizes foreign policy as a series of discrete problems, each to be approached, often in chronological order, on its own terms and on its own merits. Each such confrontation represents a miniature strategic exercise in and of itself, to be scrutinized, estimated, and addressed in a context designed to produce victory in the immediate situation of crisis. Strategic fulfillment is to be achieved not in terms of one final triumph that realizes the goal but rather by the accumulation of the fruits of a relatively large number of small victories.

The fractionating implication inherent in this notion of problem-solving has had a number of consequences. In the first place, America's policy-makers tend to treat each area of involvement as a unique strategic problem, thus robbing the nation of much of its capacity to impose priorities on itself. It is a habit of action that forces primary importance and transcendent attention upon whatever issue may be under consideration at the moment.

Second, flexibility in devising operational approaches to dissimilar problems is seldom matched by equivalent elasticity in meeting new circumstances that arise within a single crisis. The very stylistic traits that enable America to assume that each problem is a fresh strategic exercise because of accidental peculiarities of time and place seem also to require that a crisis strategy, once adopted, be pursued to the end of the problem regardless of the outcome.

Finally, the nation's insistence in tilting with crises as a basis of its foreign policy-making has served to underline its many interventions in other countries. What this has meant in practice is the belief that intervention is a useful technique for dealing with America's continuing political and socioeconomic challenges. "Trouble avoidance" and "crisis management" have become the bedrock of the nation's interventions abroad—a kind of "solutionism" that, despite its many problems, continues to exert the most powerful of holds upon the minds and hearts of America's statesmen—a mindset that would be most clearly manifested in the unfolding of the Cold War with Soviet Russia after 1945.

The Ends-Means Quandary

Before any nation can expect to be successful in maximizing its values and beliefs in the world, its statesmen must wrestle with a classic challenge: the reconciliation of ends and means. The ends of state action in international affairs—the nation's goals and objectives that it has posited for itself as best suited to translate its values into reality—are normally postulated *a priori* (ahead of time). In specific policy situations, however, one of the most recurring and enervating dilemmas policy-makers must face is the determination of an optimum relationship between abstract ends and concrete means.

Ends, at least in theory, should determine means. In a situation that may allow a number of possible courses of action, that one should be selected that most directly advances the national purpose. In practice, however, there is always a real temptation to allow means to deflect the direction of ends, to decide that those goals and objectives that are the most feasible to achieve are in fact the ones the nation should pursue. Any ambiguity or confusion in the ends-means relationship, any loss of perspective of the value roots of policy, or any failure to maintain a firm commitment to the achievement of the national purpose cannot help but deprive a foreign policy of essential meaning and effectiveness. One of the most persistent weaknesses manifested in American foreign policy over the years has been a nagging inability on the part of its decision-makers to make these sorts of distinctions. This problem may be most clearly seen in what may be called the triumph of technique in American history.

The Triumph of Technique. Flowing from its pragmatic bias, it can hardly be unexpected that one outcome of this tendency is a certain infatuation with means, a great faith in the efficacy of techniques in problem-solving. This is reflected in the tendency to quantify solutions to problems. If first you do not succeed, try again, but double and triple what it is that you are presently doing in response to the problem; hammer it into submission.

The country's special manner in dealing with foreign affairs as a series of crises has contributed to and exacerbated this quantification bias. The crisis orientation tends to undermine the nation's long-term goals by the substitution of short-term considerations, which are then all too easily rationalized as being long range. Since America's experience has indicated that agreement is normally more difficult to obtain on matters of general principle than it is on specific problems, its strategic norms have usually stressed a piece-by-piece approach to agreement and the division of the tasks of strategic action into manageable portions. There is no necessary reason in logic or in tactical doctrine why this fractionating of strategy should obscure long-term goals, but ordinary human preoccupation with the immediate as against the ultimate has often contributed, as might be expected, to exactly this outcome.

America's relationship with Soviet Russia after 1945 certainly reflected this situation. As the nation's involvement in its growing struggle with the Russian state intensified after World War II, our policy-makers became increasingly preoccupied with specific issues as they arose in a determined effort to win (or at least to avoid losing) each and every confrontation with Moscow. Defeat was regarded as a catastrophe, victory as a vindication. The result was an obscuring of long-range planning by the country as successive administrations got bogged down in successive overlays of response to the exigencies of incessant crisis.

The rise to prominence of the military in the nation's foreign policy processes in the post–Second World War era epitomizes the triumph of technique in America's foreign relations. As the military viewpoint gained in authority during these years, its spokesmen and those who accepted their judgments grew impatient with any thinking that went much beyond determination of the capabilities of others. In fact, the disproportionate influence, even hegemony, of the military in the country's foreign policy-making amounted to a victory of the capabilities school of thought over the intentions school of thought in regard to dealing with Soviet Russia. The military in this instance fell victim to the hubris to which every dominant group is prone. In such times as these it is safer and easier to avoid the effort to analyze the nuances embedded in your opponent's policy-making and to credit him indiscriminately with all sinister designs, even when some of his actions may be mutually contradictory. Once foreign policy is militarized, consideration of political subtleties tends to be shunted aside.

In this way, one comes, finally, to the resort to force that has been so highly valued in the nation's historic behavior. Born of a historic unwillingness to understand or tolerate basic conflicts of purpose, the threat or employment of force in foreign policy has become one of the most widely practiced and accepted components in the arsenal of America's problem-solving techniques. Today, manipulation of force represents the apotheosis of means in America's foreign policy.

The Appeal to Force. Violence in America has normally stemmed from the inability of its people to deal with the contradiction between the ideal of harmony that has characterized their hopes and aspirations and the specifics of real-life situations that refuse to correspond to that norm. Within America, the pragmatic style in dealing with problems has often been brilliantly productive; insofar as the nation's problems appear to have been "solved" more easily and quickly than what might be expected, the resort to force has not been so widespread. But in foreign affairs, the unsolvable—which is the norm, not the exception—brings forth the exorcising compulsion to use force.

One reason for the seeming dichotomy in the nation's domestic and foreign orientations has been the traditional habit of Americans to think in absolute rather than in discriminate terms when it comes to force—an inclination influenced by a conception of force as a single-edged weapon that ought to be drawn only in a righteous cause. This preference is due no doubt to the distance of the country from the primary source of state action over a period of many years. It was also influenced by the deep religious component in the nation's perceptual processes, leading the people very early in their collective life to develop fundamentalist, mechanical, and absolutist notions of war and peace.[17]

The idea that war and peace are separate and successive phases of policy, to be conducted by different sets of criteria, has long attracted Americans. The classic Clauswitzian conception of war as the continuation of politics by other means has not appealed very much. Indeed, it is no accident that the notion of war in American history has often had the connotation of something "special," even exotic—a self-contained exercise, expressive of a qualitatively distinct set of approaches, and associated with a psychological mindset unlike that in time of peace.[18] The concept of "cold war," with its intrinsic containment component, is perhaps the most persistent and comprehensive reflection of this view in the years after 1945.

THE AMERICAN BARGAINING STYLE

Americans think of solving problems rather than living with them. They find compromise an unnatural alternative to victory. These attitudes are a reflection of the nation's historic frontier mentality, of the cult of individualism, and of a national experience in which success is habitually regarded as the inevitable result of persistent effort. Throughout its history America has often said it would make no compromise with its principles in order to gain advantages that at best could never be more than temporary. This is partially an outgrowth of its Puritan fundamentalism with its notions of "right is right and wrong is wrong." It is also a reflection of America's moralist conception of reality and, as such, an explicit rejection of the old European concept of compromise as a mutual bargain.

In more recent years, compromise has acquired the connotation of "appeasement" in the nation's approach to problem-solving. In America's eyes, appeasement is tantamount to surrender, an outlook impregnated with immoral implications, and one that contains historical antecedents going back to the "XYZ Affair" with France[19] and the attitude displayed toward the Barbary Pirates. Then the cry was: "Millions for defense, not a penny for tribute." Later it would become: "There can be no substitute for victory."

In response to Munich in 1938, America roundly condemned the dismemberment of Czechoslovakia as "immoral" and a "sell out." The subsequent events leading to World War II seemed to confirm this conviction and became an important element in the American national tradition. We have not to this day succeeded in extricating ourselves from it. Even now, appeasement retains the suggestion of capitulation and duplicity in this country. It is in this context that America's fear of diplomacy itself may best be understood, for that ancient craft has always emphasized the central importance of compromise as its very reason for being.

Fear of Diplomacy

The notions of surrender and mendacity early became identified in the public mind with diplomacy as somehow a dissolute exercise. The puritanical suspicion of diplomacy was traditionally supported by the relative isolation of America and therefore the lack of necessity to negotiate and to compromise continually in order to survive and/or prosper.

The nation's distrust of diplomacy may also be seen in its historic philosophical rejection of Old World values and principles. Americans have been prone to classify diplomacy as a European conception, which was incompatible with the values supposedly animating American society. To the American mind, diplomacy was intimately associated with autocracy; it was the pastime of an aristocratic elite practiced to the detriment of the common people in both the Old and New Worlds. Success in diplomacy required skills—deceit, dishonesty, immorality, and dissimulation—that America believed contrasted directly with its own unique system.[20]

It is in this sense that diplomats in America's historic mindset have often been seen as "un-American," for their training and experience leads them to question the traditional self-image of American politics—the notion that ours is a unique society that the rest of the world should regard as a model for its own aspiring development. Instead, the diplomatic mode of thought suggests that other states may also have feelings of self-esteem and mission and that the "self-evident truths" of Americans are not always so evident to everyone else.

The distrust of diplomacy has another root. Not only have Americans traditionally been outraged with the immorality of power politics; they have also long entertained grave doubts about their capacity to engage successfully in it. The truth is that for a long time Americans were reluctant to put the country to the test of active, continuous engagement in the highly competitive milieu of diplomatic interactions. The obvious unease with which America approached diplomatic bargaining was clearly manifest in the years after 1945, most especially in its relations with the Soviet Russia. During the long Cold War, a world of perpetual "intolerable crisis" seemed preferable to many Americans to the possibility of being "hoodwinked by a bunch of city slickers." This suspicion of diplomacy in America is most graphically reflected in its attitude toward negotiations—the very essence of the diplomatic technique.

The Approach to Negotiations

Consider America's attitude toward negotiating with enemies. On the one hand, America's principles dictate that we should avoid confronting the nation's adversaries in spirited negotiation, since this is not the best way to handle conflicts; after all, the country's principles might be adulterated. This is a view on behalf of which some of America's greatest leaders have labored. With his constant defense of "international justice" and his unwillingness to accept realistic compromises based upon considerations of national power, Thomas Jefferson became the first in a long line of American statesmen, in the decade before America's involvement in the War of 1812, to lead his people down the path to death and destruction for the sake of universal principles accepted only by America.[21]

Woodrow Wilson, Franklin Roosevelt, Harry Truman, John Foster Dulles, Lyndon Johnson, and Ronald Reagan are among the more prominent examples of American leaders who have in this fashion drunk deeply at the well of Jeffersonian utopianism in the twentieth century. We continually fail to understand the other fellow's predicament and refuse to accept the idea that in diplomacy, in many cases, both parties are "right." Of all of America's national habits of action, this may be the one most irritating to others. Many others simply will not accept the idea that America represents truth and justice, while its adversaries are always international sinners and prevaricators. One of the best ways to create a stalemate is to go to the bargaining table armed with principles you refuse to compromise.

Consider also the belief that arrangements actually worked out with America's adversaries will probably be either misleading or without lasting value. This is a view that flows from more than the country's recent Cold War experience; it reflects a long standing conviction that there really is no "halfway house" of agreement except insofar as necessities of national security absolutely require it. But Americans are never at a loss to socialize their opponents into the values of harmony, either with offers to "sit down and reason together" or with pragmatic efforts at fractionating conflicts and issues. The end result is often greater intransigence on the part of those involved.[22]

One consequence of America's historic urge to stand on inflexible moral principle is the difficulty of retreating from a diplomatic position once assumed. A retreat would be precisely the kind of selling out that is most distasteful to

Americans—a situation that has made negotiations with enemies and allies alike a most difficult procedure, serving to postpone the settlement of outstanding international issues. A related difficulty is the obvious discomfort that America has in negotiating differences with other nations on the basis of equality. The irony here is that although American society was "born free" of the inequalities of European feudalism and the hierarchical class consciousness of post-feudal industrial society, its encounters with the rest of the world have tended to be something less than egalitarian.

In reflecting upon the nation's conception of negotiations, two conclusions are in order: It frequently complicates the nation's ability to manage its contentions rationally, and it contributes to a misunderstanding of its motives on the part of others. It has, therefore, often been more difficult for other countries' foreign policy experts to grasp the nuances of our policies than the other way around.

NOTES

1. For an extended discussion of the impact of the domestic environment on the development of the American problem-solving style, see Frederick H. Hartmann, *The New Age of American Foreign Policy* (New York: Macmillan, 1970), Chapter 2.

2. The notions of impatience and the preference for dichotomies employed in this section are inspired by Chares O. Lerche, Jr., *Foreign Policy of the American People*, 3rd ed. (Englewood Cliffs, N.J.: Prentice-Hall, 1967), Chapter 4.

3. For an excellent analysis of the potential for abuse that an uncritical resort to history entails, see Ernest R. May, *"Lessons" of the Past: The Use and Misuse of History in American Foreign Policy* (London: Oxford University Press, 1973). May, in this incisive monograph, demonstrates how reliant on historical analogies for present situations decision-makers often are. Faced with incomplete information about the immediate problem at hand, it is not surprising that policy-makers turn to the past for guidance. The crucial question is how well they are able to employ the past. May is not very optimistic: "Policy-makers," he says, "ordinarily use history badly. When resorting to an analogy, they tend to seize upon the first that comes to mind. They do not search more widely. Nor do they pause to analyze the case, test its fitness, or even ask in what ways it might be misleading. Seeing a trend running toward the present, they tend to assume that it will continue into the future, not stopping to consider what produced it or why a linear projection might prove to be mistaken" (p. xi). See also Moses I. Finlay, *The Use and Abuse of History* (New York: Viking Press, 1975).

4. The Seven Years War in Europe (1756–1763) illustrates well the basis for colonial distrust of British diplomacy and hence its subsequent preference for independence of action. The war was precipitated by a coalition of France, Russia, and Austria with the aim of punishing Prussia for its diplomatic behavior stemming from an earlier conflict, the War of the Austrian Succession. The British government supported Prussia for a variety of reasons, not the least being that Prussia was felt to be vital in the maintenance of the balance of power. The American colonists obediently fought the French in the New World (the Austrians and Russians having no

physical presence in the immediate area), although many in the colonies suspected that London was employing colonial resources and lives to achieve goals unrelated to their own well-being.

5. Spain long had grievances against the British. It had lost some territory to Britain in two earlier conflicts, Gibraltar and the Floridas being the most irksome to it, and therefore hoped to regain them. The French viewed the conflict as a way to curtail the growing power of Britain, which had reached a preeminent position by this time in the international system. For a discussion of the events of this period, see Samuel Flagg Bemis, *The Diplomacy of the American Revolution* (Bloomington: Indiana University Press, 1957); and William C. Stinchcombe, *The American Revolution and the French Alliance* (Syracuse, N.Y.: Syracuse University Press, 1969).

6. Among the best accounts of Europe's nineteenth-century balance of power arrangement are Edward Vose Gulick, *Europe's Classical Balance of Power* (Ithaca, N.Y.: Cornell University Press, 1955); Henry A. Kissinger, *A World Restored: Metternich, Castlereagh, and the Problem of Peace* (Boston: Houghton-Mifflin Co., 1957); A.J.P. Taylor, *The Struggle for the Mastery of Europe, 1848–1918* (Oxford: Clarendon Press, 1960); and C. K. Webster, *The Foreign Policy of Castlereagh* (London: G. Bell and Sons, 1947).

7. In brief, the situation involved a struggle between an effective British blockade of continental Europe and the French dictator's paper blockade of Britain: "paper" because he did not possess the capability (e. g., the navy) to enforce it. As a declared neutral anxious to trade with both countries and greatly irritated by the restrictions and harassment that both blockades represented, America was stuck in the middle. In the end, President Madison determined on war against the state that refused to lift its blockade against the other belligerent. The British declined, since their blockade was a vital weapon in their anti-French arsenal. Napoleon, on the other hand, was more than happy to suspend his blockade, which had been ineffectual anyway. The Americans, caught "between the devil and the deep blue sea," declared war on Britain.

8. One of the best works on the War of 1812 is still Bradford Perkins' *Prologue to War: England the United States, 1805–1812* (Berkeley: University of California Press, 1961). Perkins' book makes a strong case for American ineptitude in its foreign policy at the time. Although dated, a good analysis of the literature is Warren H. Goodman's "The Origins of the War of 1812: A Survey of Changing Interpretations," *Mississippi Valley Historical Review*, 28 (September, 1941), pp. 171–186. A more recent bibliography for the entire war is John C. Fredriksen, ed., *Shield of Republic/Sword of Empire: A Bibliography of U.S. Military Affairs, 1783–1846* (Westport, Conn.: Greenwood, 1990).

9. A striking example of American unilateralism during the war was Wilson's personal attempt to negotiate with Germany an end to the conflict. As the German military and economic situation rapidly deteriorated, Berlin sought talks with the American government on some sort of truce arrangement. In fact, four series of exchanges occurred between the two governments. Wilson refrained from consulting with either the British or the French while insisting to the Germans that they make a number of concessions (e. g., the abdication of the kaiser). Only when Wilson was sure that Germany was sincere in its desire to end the war did he turn the communications over to his "associates."

10. Paul Seabury, *Power, Freedom and Diplomacy: The Foreign Policy of the United States of America* (New York: Random House, 1963), p. 38.

11. On this matter, see Lerche, *Foreign Policy of the American People,* p. 111.

12. Alexis de Tocqueville, *Democracy in America,* 2, ed. Phillips Bradley (New York: Vintage Books, 1958), p. 44.

13. William James was America's foremost interpreter of pragmatism. In his own philosophical approach, James did not try to find final answers to the stubborn problems that have troubled thinkers since the ancient Greeks. Instead, he urged men to choose beliefs that would help them to lead active, successful lives. If a belief in God made people happy, James argued, it was not important whether or not God really existed. The later "instrumentalism" of John Dewey, a kind of refinement of the original conception of pragmatism, argued that it is in their relative contributions to the improvement of human society where one may find the criterion for evaluating the work of competing philosophies and/or political belief systems.

14. Kenneth Keniston, *The Uncommitted* (New York: Harcourt, Brace, 1965), p. 254.

15. While this is not the place for any extensive commentary on the implications of the pragmatic approach for problem-solving in America's domestic affairs, the nation's cities manifest the worst side effects of an overindulgent pragmatism: overcrowding, pollution, rampant crime, squalor, disease, and decay. New York City in the last two decades of the twentieth century was a good case in point. The underground brick pipelines used to carry water to the city from its distant reservoirs were so antiquated that millions of gallons of the precious fluid were leaking out into the ground annually. The city decided to do nothing about it because it would cost too much money to check for the leaks. Then there was the city's subway system. In an age of unprecedented high-rise office buildings and sophisticated computers, that transportation network was judged to have an electrical system fit only for display in a museum. A nation that prides itself on getting to Europe faster with more people per airplane finds that it takes almost as long to get to and from the airport. The enormous accomplishments in highway construction, spurred on by the nation's great love of the automobile, have now become one of endless duplication, while the desperate need for a carefully planned mass transit system remains unfulfilled—not even seriously addressed. But perhaps the most poignant illustration is the overbearing redundancy that has been built into government bureaucracy in this country, particularly at the federal level. Programs that were initially developed in a pragmatic spirit in response to specific problems are not only retained long after their usefulness is finished, but become entrenched in the body politic, while improvisations on the same themes are grafted onto the older ones, or layered in a stifling array dotting the landscape. The list is virtually endless, and the prospects of genuine remediation go begging in the absence of a national commitment to systematic rethinking.

For an excellent treatment of the pragmatic spirit in America's foreign relations, see Cecil V. Crabb, Jr., *American Diplomacy and the Pragmatic Tradition* (Baton Rouge: Louisiana State University Press, 1989).

16. Reinhold Niebuhr and Alan Heimert, *A Nation So Conceived* (New York: Charles Scribner's Sons, 1963), p. 150.

17. The seventeenth-century Puritan fanatic Richard Sibbes, for example,

advocated "a holy violence" to rid Britain of a corrupt religious-political order. See J. C. Brauer, *Reflections on the Nature of English Puritanism* (Boston: Beacon Press, 1954), p. 102.

18. America's periodic domestic forays or "wars" against poverty, disease, and crime immediately come to mind. It is interesting to recall that Senator Hubert H. Humphrey, in seeking a catch phrase with which to label his proposals to deal with the problems of the nation's urban areas, once borrowed from President Truman's Secretary of State: What we need, he said, was a "Marshall Plan" for the cities.

19. The matter of Messrs. XYZ arose in the context of a protracted effort by President John Adams in 1800 to maintain the country's neutrality at a time when the British and the French were at war. The French had been raiding American ships, stirring up a warlike atmosphere in America. Adams sent a three-man diplomatic mission to Paris to arrange a treaty. There, the diplomats were visited by three agents of the French foreign minister Talleyrand. These agents, known as X, Y, and Z, asked for a bribe of $240,000. When news of this episode reached America, it caused an uproar and led to an undeclared war between the two countries. Realizing the country was not strong enough to fight the French Empire, Adams, despite immense pressure, persisted in his efforts for peace, which was finally achieved by the Convention of 1800.

20. John Adams, for example, was convinced that Americans could never be a match for European diplomats who would resort to any device to achieve their ends.

21. For a provocative accounting of Jefferson's culpability in the onset of the War of 1812, see Melwin Small, *Was War Necessary? National Security and U. S. Entry into War* (Beverly Hills, Calif.: Sage Publications, 1980), Chapter 1. For a worthwhile overview of the Jeffersonian approach to foreign relations, see Lawrence S. Kaplan, *American Foreign Policy in the Age of Jefferson* (Kent, Ohio: Kent State University Press, 1987).

22. This attitude toward negotiations was particularly manifest in the country's approach to dealing with the Vietminh in the 1960s and 1970s. The Geneva discussions during those years represent a textbook study of the difficulties inherent in America's problem-solving orientation. See, in this vein, George Herring, "The War in Vietnam," in Robert Divine, ed., *Exploring the Johnson Years* (Austin: University of Texas Press, 1981); Allan Goodman, *The Lost Peace: America's Search for a Negotiated Settlement of the Vietnam War* (Palo Alto, Calif.: Hoover Institute, 1978); and David Kraslow and Stuart Loory, *The Secret Search for Peace in Vietnam* (New York: Random House, 1968). For a broader perspective, see also Doris Kearns, *Lyndon Johnson and the American Dream* (New York: Harper, 1976). On the difficulties of bargaining, most especially that of accurately communicating one's positions to the other side, see Roger Fisher, *International Conflict for Beginners*, rev. ed., (Boston: Peter Smith Publishers, 1985).

CHAPTER 4

The Isolationist-
Interventionist Impulse

The oldest lesson in history is the futility and, often, fatality of foreign
interference to maintain in power a government unwanted or hated at home.
—Barbara Tuchman

The history of American foreign policy from the earliest days of the Republic
has reflected a rather remarkable composite of two seemingly contradictory
orientations—isolationism and interventionism. It is a record in which these
two policy imperatives have amounted to a kind of "unity of opposites" in our
history.

At first glance it might seem somewhat incongruous to speak of
America's "isolationist-interventionist" impulse. Isolationism, at least among
America's elites, if not always in the popular consciousness, is generally
conceived of as something out of America's past—dead and gone—an approach
that, while perhaps appropriate at earlier points in time, is neither a viable
policy option any longer nor a reflection of the nation's real needs and desires.
Interventionism, on the other hand, is viewed today by many people, whatever
their disagreements about specifics, as a function of America's great power role
in contemporary international affairs. The "containment" doctrine, which in its
various guises underlay much of America's post-1945 role, was frequently
viewed in this context as a kind of encapsulation of the country's mandatory
realist political style in the last half of the century. If isolationism was the
midwife of the past, interventionism, it is said, is the handmaiden of the present.

While superficially appealing, this characterization misses the point.
America's historically manifested isolationism and its propensity for
interventionism represent two sides of the same coin—each oft displayed in the
nation's conduct. Whatever its appropriateness may have been in the past, the
isolationist-interventionist orientation has been one very important way in
which America has comprehended and related to the complications of the real

world. Isolationism is an instinct of withdrawal—a rejection of the world's complexity. Interventionism is this impulse turned inside out—a wish to end complexity by transforming the world through the benevolent action of a well-meaning America. In their joint vision of a truly peaceful world, the two orientations incorporate a specifically American dream. Each rejects reality, the world as it is, though in different ways.

The importance of this orientation in America's relationship to the rest of mankind cannot be overemphasized. The historical legacy of its isolationist–interventionist duopoly has provided America's decision-makers with remarkably durable precedents for very dissimilar policies over the years. The isolationist-interventionist impulse, viewed from this perspective, is as relevant today for the making and carrying out of American foreign policy as it was at the onset of our national existence.

THE ISOLATIONIST INSTINCT

One of the most persistent of America's habits of action has been the commitment to the isolationist position in world affairs. No other orientation has meant more to America, has more deeply touched the "soul" of the American character, or has so persistently reflected the hopes of its people than has the isolationist impulse. As a policy imperative manifested throughout the course of American history, it ranks at the very highest level in the hierarchy of America's foreign policy postures. For more than a century and a half—from the time it declared its independence in 1776 until Pearl Harbor—a foreign policy of isolation was viewed by most Americans as a necessary condition for their national security, a guarantee of the future success of their democratic experiment, and an important foundation of their social stability and economic well-being. In short, to the doorstep of the isolationist rationale, Americans historically tended to ascribe all the benefits conferred by the successful pursuit of the American way of life.

Departure from the policy of isolation, it was thought, invited a host of potential dangers: foreign interference in the domestic affairs of the nation; militarism; an erosion of the freedoms guaranteed by the Bill of Rights; the possibility of presidential dominance, even dictatorship, at the expense of the powers of the Congress, not to mention the internal divisiveness and political factionalism that would surely follow.

In the early nineteenth century, Secretary of State John Quincy Adams succinctly summarized for his fellow citizens why American interference in the affairs of others should be rejected and how isolation might best be practiced:

Wherever the standard of freedom and independence has been or shall be unfurled, there will America's heart, her benedictions, and her prayers be. But she goes not abroad in search of monsters to destroy. She is the well-wisher to the freedom and independence of all. She is the champion and vindicator of her own. She will recommend the general cause by the countenance of her voice, and by the benignant sympathy of her example. Otherwise she might become the dictatress of the world. She would no longer be the ruler of her spirit.[1]

Thus, if America was to be involved in the world, it was to be a passive involvement at best. America, in terms of this tradition, was not to assume responsibility for the world, even in the name of freedom. Instead of active involvement, the nation's role was to be one of restraint, of moderation, of repudiation of the kind of militant policy that, the Founding Fathers feared, would only subvert cherished ideals, undermine the unique promise of the American vision, and ultimately, jeopardize the preservation of freedom in America itself.

It is no accident that the concept has frequently exerted a great attraction for the country's intellectuals. Charles Beard, for example, was convinced that under the shelter provided by this doctrine "human beings were set free to see what they could do on this continent, when emancipated from the privilege-encrusted institutions of Europe and from entanglements in the endless revolutions and wars of that continent."[2] Foreign observers have been no less fascinated with it. Lord Bryce, that wise commentator on the American scene, was once moved to say that "America lives in a world of her own. . . . Safe from attack, safe from menace, she hears from afar the warring cries of European races and faiths. . . . But for the present at least—it may not always be so—she sails upon a summer sea."[3]

In the years after 1945 the influence of the isolationist urge would not disappear. The nation's more or less consistent adherence to this isolationist stance for the first 150 years of its national existence deeply impacted the American approach to foreign relations after World War II. Today, while fewer Americans perhaps subscribe to an avowedly isolationist position, many of the assumptions, preconceptions, popular images, attitudes, and sentiments associated with the isolationist impulse remain deeply entrenched in the American psyche and continue to affect the thinking of the American people and the policy-making of their leaders.

Isolationism Defined

Isolationism is a complex phenomenon, not a very simple concept to delineate.[4] A remarkable attribute of the concept has been its richness and adaptability. Throughout the course of American history, the concept took on a number of implications, not all of which have been always mutually consistent or compatible. Isolationism has in fact historically represented a configuration of attitudes and assumptions about America's proper relationship with the outside world. During no period of American history did isolationism constitute a rational, internally consistent set of foreign policy principles. On the contrary, the substance of isolationism tended to vary from period to period. Indeed, from the time of Washington's Farewell Address to the present, there has been more of a tendency for isolationism to be conceived in terms of the *concrete* policy issues confronting America at any given moment in its foreign and domestic affairs—a reflection of the nation's pragmatic spirit.

Isolationist thought has existed on several levels in the nation's history. For some Americans, it has captured the essence of America's geographic distance from other nations, especially from the peoples of Europe. There is no question that isolationism was partially derived from the country's geographic separation from the Old World and the earliest Americans' concomitant absorption in creating and developing a new civilization. For others, it stressed America's spiritual and philosophical segregation from the European continent, underlining the dissimilarity between the "progressive" American way of life and Europe's "stagnant" social and economic systems.

In this same vein, many Americans were long fond of drawing attention to what they regarded as fundamental political and ideological distinctions between the democracy of the New World and the despotic authoritarianisms and corrupt political systems of the Old. It is this conception of the meaning and importance of America's isolationist orientation that perhaps comes closest to the primordial character of the American people. Americans were isolationists because they wanted to wrench themselves from the Old World once and for all and to make clear their differences, for the whole sense of the nation's cultural self-identity has been bound up with the idea that America is a unique society, a new society, of necessity, a post-European society.

Here was the typical American's perception of his nation as a "new dispensation" made most clearly manifest. It was as if, by founding the Republic, and maintaining it inviolate from the sins of the world, Americans had created a new covenant with the Maker. Few policies among the politics of nations have ever been more closely attuned than American isolationism to the sources of a country's comprehension of its role in the world. In this sense it must be seen, ultimately, not as a political doctrine at all, although certainly political in form. It is to be understood, at bottom, as a quintessentially moral role. Only in America could we say with the song: "Humanity with all its fears, with all the hopes of future years is hanging breathless on thy fate."

Certainly, a basic component of the isolationist impulse was the idea—the conviction—that the solution of major domestic problems had first claim upon the energies and resources of the American people. Because Americans from the beginning had to contend with a host of environmental challenges associated with the settlement of a vast continent, and the evolution of viable political and economic arrangements, there came very early to exist a natural preoccupation with domestic affairs. The tradition of Americans being interested in those things that were close to them in either space or time rapidly grew into an ingrained habit of thought. The very fact that the citizens of the rest of the world were for a long time rather far away contributed to this outlook. The well-known apathy and antipathy of the American people toward foreign affairs may be traced back to this primacy of domestic affairs in the lives of America's people. Today, of course, the world is not as far away as it once was;

still, the immediacy of international affairs is rarely as great for most Americans as that of local, state, or national ones—except, that is, in moments of perceived crisis.[5]

Another component of the isolationist credo was an insistence upon America's non-involvement in foreign wars. America's eagerness to avoid such conflicts was no mere abstraction emanating from the mouths of the country's Founding Fathers. It was a resolve that developed from the American people's experience during the colonial period and the early years under the Constitution. Between 1689 and 1815 England and France went to war seven times, fighting each other for almost half of that 126 year period. Americans were involved in some fashion or other in every one of these conflict situations, regardless of their own desires in the matter. Is it any wonder that in the years leading up to the American Revolution the benefits to be had from non involvement in Europe's wars were seen as one of the main benefits of "separation" from England.[6]

The fear of unwanted involvement in foreign wars not of our own making was the major contributing factor to perhaps the most widely recognized definition of isolationism in American history: the idea of diplomatic and military non-entanglement. From the Washington administration down to the Second World War, the view that America, for security purposes, must remain free from complicating commitments to the Old World was a hallowed viewpoint for most Americans. The injunction against entangling alliances came over time to be universalized and sanctified into a kind of rule. It is also in this particular guise that the isolationist impulse should be seen as an attempt to preserve the national sovereignty of America, including its independence in policy-making. Although, as we shall point out, the tendency was to interpret and apply the impulse far more rigidly and indiscriminately than its early advocates intended, the principle was enunciated, after all, in response to a particular set of circumstances that appeared to threaten the security and well being of the young and vulnerable nation—the events surrounding the onset of the French Revolution in 1789 and the subsequent rise of Napoleon Bonaparte as a threat to the European status quo.

These, then, represent the dominant intellectual and psychological ingredients of America's isolationist style *in terms of America's self-image.* The qualities of action reflective of that style would be played out on many stages over the years. But as is so often true in history, the actual development and operation of the isolationist impulse were products of somewhat more complex interactive factors.

The Isolationist Impulse in Historical Perspective

While it is certainly accurate to say that the isolationist impulse, in all of its various guises, reflected some of the most deeply held hopes and desires of the American people, the relative success of the country's decision-makers in maintaining America's independence of action and non-involvement in Europe's conflicts—indeed, in upholding the pristine inviolability of its Puritan soul—was due less to any exceptional skill or even to the validity of its premises than to circumstances.

A key point in an understanding of this reality is to remember when America came into being as a sovereign state. This country is the only great power in the world today whose early formulative history unfolded so conspicuously in the novel, unprecedented century between 1815 and 1914.[7] In the entire history of the nation state system, there has never been so prolonged a period of general peace as there was during these years. As historian C. Van Woodard has noted, until the First World War, America was "blessed with a security so complete and so free that it was able virtually to do without an army and for the greater part of the period without a navy as well."[8] The nation was involved in very few military engagements in a century distinguished by its worldwide great power peacefulness, and what few conflicts it did prosecute, it "won" easily. There can be little doubt that the ability of America to "choose" its wars was closely tied in to the operation of the nineteenth-century European balance of power system.

When President James Monroe, in December 1823, delivered his famous message to the Congress, it was an audacious undertaking on the part of the young Republic to tell Britain to stay out of the Western Hemisphere. Nevertheless, the success of the infantile American nation in both keeping others out of its hair and in staying out of theirs was due less to its own efforts than it was to the conscious, deliberate decisions of successive British governments over a period of almost a century to "enforce" the doctrine in their own national interest.

Indeed, the international strategic situation throughout the nineteenth century facilitated America's isolationist proclivities. Although the European balance of power was altered somewhat during the nation's civil war period, it did not change to its disadvantage. And as the great military-technological revolution got under way during the 1850s, making it now possible for long-range military efforts to be carried out, the balance of power situation in Europe, fortunately for America, did not permit it.

It should also be remembered that America's traditional isolationism never approximated the virtual total withdrawal into itself in the manner of Japan of the seventeenth and eighteenth centuries. At no time during these years was America wholly isolated from the rest of the world, either economically, politically, or militarily, as the nation expanded across a continent in a space of little more than sixty years, had the second largest commercial fleet in the world by 1862, and acquired an empire by the end of the nineteenth century. During the course of that century, America supported—and even helped to finance—many nationalist revolutions in the world. This was not exactly isolationism strictly defined. The impulse should be seen for what it was: a selective involvement in the economic and political arena of international politics *as America's capabilities permitted.* Except for the 1920s and 1930s,

American isolationism as policy was virtually a direct function of that capability; as its capability grew, its isolationism, *as policy*, declined.

Isolationism Recapitulated: An Assessment

In retrospect, the original policy of separation from Europe, general non involvement in its interstate relationships, and above all, non participation in its wars was both necessary and wise. There was no other sensible attitude to have taken toward Europe in the early days of the nation. America was weak, its national unity was beset by sectional rivalry, its population was small, and disdainful monarchs snarled at it from across the Atlantic. For many years after 1815 it would have been foolish to have disturbed the existing balance of power. America needed time to build a seedbed to absorb its immigrants, to subdue its thorny wasteland, to build a national loyalty that superseded regional allegiances, to settle its domestic schism, to save the Union. In this sense, nineteenth-century isolationism was salutary, expressive of a pragmatic wisdom.

Other benefits that can be attached to America's isolationist orientation prior to World War II might include historically a very low level of military expenditures, the lack of need to construct costly fortifications along its two long, lengthy borders with Canada and Mexico, and in the absence of creditable foreign threats, the ability to employ the army for internal security purposes such as the pacification of the western Indians. And while it did not preclude all partisan or internal discords over foreign policy questions, isolationist principles served a very useful role in defusing the potentially destructive impact of minority group activism in the foreign policy process. Any deviation from the isolationist stance was almost guaranteed to provoke intense ethnic and other interest group opposition.   Down to World War II, isolationism was thus important for the maintenance of internal unity, social cohesiveness, and domestic political stability.[9]   Indeed, it is difficult to think of any other foreign policy orientation that could have made a similar contribution. Nevertheless, while the isolationist impulse may be seen to be a kind of "strength proceeding from weakness" during the early decades of the Republic, it came, ultimately, in the twentieth century to plague the American people as they took up their new role as a major player in world politics.

When World War I burst like a bombshell on a psychologically adolescent America, its people were not prepared. Americans, even more than their European counterparts, had assumed that the technological advances of the previous half century had largely invalidated the game of "power politics." The procedures of state craft were not comprehended in Washington; it never dawned on America's decision makers that it was the European balance of power that had preserved the peace or that it was British sea power that had underwritten American security. President Wilson and the American decision-making elite became aware of the balance of power—particularly the significance of its alliance component—only at the very end of an equilibrist system that on the whole had represented the most impressive peace preserving mechanism devised by man up to that time.[10] But in the final days of the equilibrist system, the balancing mechanism seemed to represent entanglements pervaded by selfish rivalries.

America was simply not ready in 1917—nor would it be in 1940–41—to be productively involved in the mainstream of international affairs. Its leaders did not know how to participate fully or even to determine what the nation's most appropriate role should be. Isolationism was hardly conducive to the diplomatic training of a national people about to emerge as a world power. Competent and experienced diplomats were few and far between in major posts abroad until the 1930s. The reason was unambiguously clear: Relatively little importance was attached to the job from the standpoint of the national welfare. Indeed, most of the normal tools of foreign policy, from the minuscule career diplomatic service to the truncated armed forces, certainly testify to a nation not especially troubled by external threats to its national security. The picture is rounded out with the realization that no attention at all was paid to intelligence operations during these years.

Moreover, as many observers have noted, the apparent success of the isolationist imperative tended to confirm Americans in a tendency to profess an uncritical, easygoing faith in the utility of words, of presidential pronouncements, in signed documents to achieve diplomatic purposes.[11] Persuaded, for example, that it was merely the proclamation of the Monroe Doctrine by an American president rather than a desire by the British to honor it that underwrote its success, it was not difficult for Americans thereafter to equate the assertion of a policy or the mere expression of good intentions with their achievement.

After World War I the continuing attractiveness of isolationism tended to mislead Americans with regard to the real foundations of their national security and the steps required to maintain it. As a consequence of this pervasive confidence in the isolationist credo, America abrogated its national defense responsibilities after World War I. Perhaps more than any other period of American history, the 1920s and 1930s were characterized by the existence of debilitating assumptions concerning the bases of American security in a rapidly changing global environment. We refused to play a role in the League of Nations. Instead of utilizing the military option in a selective and judicious manner, as events necessitated, for the purpose of maintaining international peace, the country was satisfied to rely upon "moral force" and global public opinion as the primary bases for the preservation of a benign global order. It did not turn out that way, of course, and much of the substance of post-1945 American foreign policy would be an attempt to apply an appropriate corrective to the "unrealism" of this era.

One can also not avoid the observation that America's ingrained suspicion of foreign governments—sometimes manifesting itself in a kind of obtuse if not xenophobic, nationalism—has helped to sustain this country's isolationist instinct historically. In America's psychological repudiation of Old World values and principles, in its oft-expressed conviction that traditional diplomacy is suspect, it has been but one more step to assume that entanglements overseas simply are not beneficial to the American way of life. Even after America emerged as a superpower, public interest in foreign affairs remained low and fragile.[12] In this way, the isolationist impulse served as both an expression and a reinforcement of the traditional distrust of power politics inherent in the Puritan Ethic. For Americans to involve themselves in a game where the players' intellects have been perceived to dominate their moral faculties is simply not palatable.

It is also well to remember that the popularity of the isolationist ethic, with its roots deeply impacted by the nation's fear of power politics, has had another source—what we have already referred to as America's sense of inadequacy. Americans consequently have liked nothing better than to escape from the bad guys altogether, to be done with it. This has tended to be translated into the view, even today, that one must reduce one's contacts, limit one's kinds of participation, and/or control the relationships of any involvement in the system. But there is a great distinction between a policy of self-restraint, which still seeks to affect the world of events but determines that the most fruitful outcome is one achieved by a watchful low profile, and an urge to "pack it in." The former is a policy; the latter is not. Self-restraint is responsibility; withdrawal is its neglect.

In the post-1945 era, at a time in which America felt it necessary to bear the cross of international commitment, the isolationist impulse would not vanish. It continues to be expressed on one side by those who hold an abiding nostalgia for the old isolationist days, when internal matters were the overriding political concern, and who anticipate the moment when America can withdraw from commitment. It is shared on the other side by many who would prefer the nation tend its own affairs within a "fortress America"—a mighty force that can be brought into play as necessary but that would refrain from tangible commitment. It remains a deeply felt, instinctive response that troubles and haunts America's role in the contemporary world.[13]

THE INTERVENTIONIST SYNDROME

In the midst of the nation's preferred foreign policy posture of isolationism there has existed a corresponding reality, part and parcel of what Cecil Crabb, Jr. calls "the essentially paradoxical or dual nature of the American outlook toward foreign affairs."[14] From the onset of the American state, the long era of isolationist behavior was interspersed with overt interventionist episodes. While somewhat infrequent and episodic earlier in the nation's history, these activities prefigured the activist, globalist interventionism of America's foreign policy after 1945.[15]

Yet the seeming conflict between America's traditional isolationist impulse and its interventionist proclivities has been more apparent than real. In the American mind, their ultimate goals have been substantially identical: to create the necessary conditions in the outside world for the achievement of America's national purpose. While the isolationist impulse has emphasized the necessity of stressing the American "example" and non-involvement in order to *encourage* the necessary conditions abroad for the achievement of its national purpose, the interventionist urge has stressed the need to take an active, involved posture in the world arena in order to *produce* that situational context necessary for the achievement of the hopes and aspirations of the American people.

America's historical interventionism has had three major sources, each reflecting in its turn a qualitatively distinct form or approach. The earliest manifestation was its physical expansionism—a constantly moving territorial frontier that inevitably involved the nation in direct confrontations with other countries. A second form of this interventionism stemmed from what may be called America's "liberal political faith"—the notion that America's belief in democracy, freedom, and equality could and must be translated into behavior overseas calculated to safeguard or to promote those values considered integral to the American way of life. After World War II, it was seen as an ongoing attempt to preserve and maintain an international status quo—a world environment that, for all its dangers and threats, America found intrinsically satisfying—against the threat perceived to be emanating from Soviet Russia and its allies. Each of these underlying motivations for the nation's historic interventionist tendencies has, in its own manner, overlapped and reinforced the others, despite a number of internal contradictions.

America's Expansionism

"The thrust of expansionism," Max Lerner has noted, "has been a continuous impulse in American history."[16] For William Appleman Williams, "expansion lies at the center of the American *Weltanschauung*. It was and remains the key to resolving the visceral problems created by the sense of uniqueness, the commitment to mission, and the way out of being isolated—of being alone."[17] Whatever one's views of the causal forces behind the territorial expansion of the nation, for a new and weak state, America proved especially vigorous in extending its borders during the first decades of independence.[18] At its inception, America was already the second largest geographical state in the world, surpassed only by Russia. Still hemmed in by European powers in 1789, America broke out of its containment and, within the space of just sixty-four years, more than doubled in size. That territorial aggrandizement continued, in fits and starts, until by the eve of the Second World War, America had acquired more than 3.7 million square miles, overseas possessions and territories accounting for about 19 percent of that total.[19]

During these years, the posture of isolationism toward other countries was not deemed incompatible with a policy of continental expansion and annexation of certain external territories like Alaska, Hawaii, the Philippines, and scattered islands in the Caribbean. Regions bordering on America were automatically regarded as part of its sphere of influence. Without undue scruples or repugnance, it engaged in the art of recruiting satellites within these zones, instigating revolts against uncooperative governments, even by the use of force when necessary.[20]   Indeed, one of the principal benefits of the country's isolationist mentality may have been its facilitation of this expansionist process by enabling Americans to devote primary attention to their own backyard.

There is little question that the doctrine of Manifest Destiny was a primary rationalization employed by the nation for its expansion across the continent and later into the world beyond. An excellent illustration of this type of thinking may be seen at the end of the nineteenth century in the debate over whether to annex the Philippines just then acquired from Spain as the result of its war with America. A kind of synthesis of the expansionist component of interventionism, the messianic mission of America to save the world and some of the more unsavory aspects of the Puritan Ethic may be seen in a speech of Senator Albert Beveridge from Indiana at the time:

Mr. President, the times call for candor. The Philippines are ours forever, territory belonging to the United States as the Constitution calls them.   We shall not repudiate our duty in the archipelago. We will not abandon our opportunity in the Orient. We will not renounce our part in the mission of our race, trustee under God, of the civilization of the world. And we will move forward to our work, not howling our regrets but with gratitude for a task worthy of our strength, and thanksgiving to Almighty God that He marked us as His chosen people, henceforth to lead in the regeneration of the world.[21]

American diplomatic history is replete with numerous instances of the nation's willingness to engage in expansionist endeavors to suit its own purposes. The fate of America's resident Indians was certainly a direct result of this propensity. In this sense, Manifest Destiny was little more than a crude euphemism for and rationalization of a policy of expulsion and extermination against what was in contemporary terminology a collection of "non-state nations." [22]

The 1840s represented the "golden age" of American expansion, a period in which America obtained from both Mexico and Britain huge chunks of territory. After the Civil War, America turned its attention to Central and South America as a matter of right. In this, the Monroe Doctrine was conceived as something more than just the defense of the hemisphere against European penetration.[23] Little by little, beginning in the Caribbean and extending gradually southward, an increasing measure of American control over Latin America became apparent under the protective umbrella of the Doctrine. So far had this gone by 1885 that Secretary of State Olney could claim that "the United States is practically sovereign on this continent, and its fiat is law upon the subjects to which it confines its interposition.[24]   America's performance in this vein extended well into the twentieth century, reaching its apogee in the first two decades of the period.

It was the American victory over the decaying monarchy of Spain that signaled the arrival of America at the level of a great power.[25] As a result of this brief and in many ways sordid conflict in which victory was obtained in a veritable comic-opera atmosphere, America succeeded to what was left of Spain's world position: a colonial empire in the Western Hemisphere and a position as a major power in the Pacific. There were two major territorial acquisitions (Puerto Rico and the Philippines) and several smaller ones (Guam and Wake Islands in the Pacific) that represented the spoils of this "splendid little war."

Cuba, the ostensible pretext for the war, achieved only partial independence; in a compromise between the "no-annexation" Democrats and the country's expansionists, the island became an American protectorate under the terms of the "Platt Amendment" of 1901. With the acquisition and occupation of advanced bases in Cuba and Puerto Rico, American influence in the Caribbean became paramount beyond any doubt. Operating from these bases, President Theodore Roosevelt in the first decade of the twentieth century was to find it relatively easy to maneuver the winning of the Panama Canal Zone from a hapless Colombia. The concomitant addition of the "Roosevelt Corollary" to the Monroe Doctrine at this time represented a goodly measure of economic imperialism and the penetration of other nations through foreign investment and trade.[26]

No element of American foreign policy received such unanimous acceptance by the public or a more solid place in tradition than the principle that America should be absolutely dominant in the Western Hemisphere. In terms of the interaction of doctrine and historical practice, the American interest in the Western Hemisphere consisted of three related concerns—concerns that remain paramount today:

All non-American states must be excluded from the hemisphere except for the remaining minor colonial holdings of Britain, France, and the Netherlands.

No real rivals in the region will be tolerated, the hemisphere being regarded as an American preserve in which Washington reigns unchallenged.

The countries of the region are to be organized into a single more or less cohesive arrangement under American leadership.[27]

In looking at the American performance in the world during these years, most of its people today would probably reject the insulting implication that imperialism constituted any part of that record. The word and the idea fly in the face of what has been held to be the "different" international role of America. Yet Americans did get caught up in the exhilarating "contest" for overseas possessions that tended to characterize the conduct of all the great powers at this time, and a rationale for the nation's expansionist policies became incorporated inevitably into the American tradition.

Although the American empire was never particularly large, in its acquisition and exploitation Americans revealed a common characteristic of an imperial people—one of rationalizing their colonizing mission as an act of philanthropy.[28] America's self-proclaimed purpose in seizing these territories was to "prepare the way" for these "unfortunate" peoples. Nevertheless, what was most revealing about the American imperial role was the fact that many Americans took seriously their verbalizations of the right of self-determination for these peoples. The record reveals a continuous, although unevenly effective, attempt to live up to their repeated claims of goodwill. The more "civilized" colonies—Puerto Rico, Hawaii, and the Philippines—were prepared for self-government; the more "backward" peoples became the objects of a host of programs of betterment. In this effort the American people were responding to a genuine urge sincerely reflective of the nation's national purpose.

Moreover, America's expansionism was always a fitful exercise at best, an enterprise in which many Americans were not especially at ease. The record of America's acquisition of empire is one accompanied with frequent outbursts of guilty conscience on the part of many of its citizens, and severe criticism directed at the corrupting effects that such empire had wrought upon the American soul. Imperialism as an all-too-familiar manifestation of power politics seemed to many people to be something that the American political genius was constitutionally incapable of carrying off successfully. It is therefore supremely ironic that the evident discontent with which so many Americans viewed the country's gaining of empire must be measured in the context of the equally prevalent propensity of Americans to intervene abroad on behalf of their democratic principles.

The Liberal Motivation

From the earliest moments after Independence, America evinced a clear tendency to project abroad in its relationships with others the basic tenets of its "liberal" democratic faith.[29] This generally took the form of seeking support for the ideals of freedom in equality, to promote democracy abroad, and to uplift the condition of the human race. Well before the dawn of the twentieth century, innumerable opportunities arose for America to interject these ideals into other lands. Hardly had the battles of Lexington and Concord ended when the effects of the American Revolution began to exert an impact in Europe. The "shots heard around the world" had a profound influence upon France, helping to trigger the revolutionary upheaval there in 1789. The ideals of 1776 were certainly considered exportable; indeed, in the early years of the Republic, it was not uncommon for the American embassy in almost every European capital to be viewed as a hotbed of subversion by their governments.[30]

Liberal interventionist sentiments also in some measure accounted for the issuance of the Monroe Doctrine in 1823. Whatever else it was, that pronouncement was surely a document in praise of the democratic principle, trumpeting democratic procedures in contrast to the authoritarian monarchies of

Europe. The Doctrine tacitly committed America to an interventionist position in a number of ways. Preventing the Holy Alliance (the arrangement among England, France, Austria, and Russia, which was then the dominant political configuration in Europe) from intervening in Latin America, and Russia from expanding in the Northwest, would, it was felt, contribute to the preservation and extension of democratic systems throughout the New World.

It would also in some measure thwart and over time, Americans believed, turn back efforts by the European powers to impose the idea of monarchical legitimacy upon reluctant subjects. This was, after all, the beginning of a rising popular outcry throughout much of Europe for freedom and self-determination. In this fashion Monroe's famous declaration expressed both opposition to European-style imperialism as Americans themselves conceived of it and a peculiarly American imperial mission as non-Americans have seen it in the Western Hemisphere. As America expanded toward the Pacific, reassured by the rhetoric of Monroe's formulation, any and all expansion could become, in the idiom of Andrew Jackson and James K. Polk, a glorious exercise in extending "the area of freedom."

The century from 1815 to World War I witnessed many episodes in which the American nation manifested liberal interventionist proclivities. In reaction to the long series of nationalist uprisings that marked the record of European politics during these years, America responded with frequent outbursts of outrage, enthusiastic public support for the suppressed peoples involved, and generous private, if only occasional public, financial support for those in need. Whether the issue was the Greek struggle for independence from Turkish rule in the 1820s, the fight in the 1830s and 1840s by the Poles and other peoples of East-Central Europe to win freedom from Russia or Austria, the revolutionary upsurge in 1848 involving many diverse segments of the European population, the Italian struggle for national unification, or most especially, the long fight by Hungarian patriots for freedom against Austrian suppression, intervention on the behalf of these forces was a logical, natural, and perhaps inevitable outgrowth of the American democratic ethos—an accurate reflection of its long-standing national purpose.[31]

American involvement both in China and in Latin America before World War II had an important liberal interventionist component, although partly explainable in the former case in economic terms, and in the latter instance in terms of America's expansionist proclivities. In each of these situations—the missionary effort in the case of China, and the desire by Wilson and others to see democracy triumph in Mexico and elsewhere in the Caribbean—the democratic, progressive, and reformist impulses in America were instrumental in providing an important basis for a series of American interventions.[32] Throughout the interwar period, the democratic interventionist dogma had much to do with America's frequent involvements in the Caribbean region, although the end result was often to put in power or to shore up indigenous regimes whose commitment to freedom or democracy was suspect at the very least. It would not be until after the 1933 Montevideo Conference that the American liberal interventionist urge in the Western Hemisphere would begin to be curbed in the context of a growing Latin American desire to hem in the "colossus to the north."[33]

There was no question that the progressive notion of equality in freedom was a major fueling factor in America's interventionism after 1940. That interventionism stemmed initially from the strong anti-colonial propensity of Franklin Roosevelt and, later to a lesser degree, that of the Truman administration. The conviction that America should use its influence to promote democracy in other countries was a view that flowed from the universalist assumption that there is an intrinsic relationship between the spread of democracy in the world and the preservation of peace, law, and order all over the globe. From here it was but a short step to the notion that America should hinder and in some cases actively oppose wherever possible anti-democratic political movements and regimes abroad.

Roosevelt's "Four Freedoms" pronouncement was a resounding call for the renewal of this interventionist orientation. The message's evocation of America's commitment to these freedoms served notice on the world that henceforth others would be expected to move resolutely down that path. Just how important these statements were as guides for America's postwar conduct cannot be underestimated. Thus, by the eve of America's involvement in the Second World War, the moral purity of America's isolationism was already giving way to the moral self-justification of the liberal basis of its intervention in the world that would characterize an important segment of its thinking during and after the war—a mode of thought and habit of action that would come, in time, to jeopardize America's success in that postwar universe.

Promotion of the Status Quo

America, as we have noted, was for a long time a revisionist state in terms of the substance of its policies and in fact remains so today by implication in terms of the social consequences of its abundance. This has not prevented it from intervening in the affairs of other nations to maintain what can only be called its present advantageous position. In the years since the acquisition of empire in the war against Spain, the nation's policy-makers, acting in harmony with popular attitudes as they understood them, have chosen more often than not to concentrate on the defense of the nation's satiated condition.

Although we shall not in this book engage in any detailed review and examination of the nation's post-1945 interventionism on behalf of the status quo, there are a number of crucial assumptions underlying that record that may be usefully addressed here. On the one hand, there is no question that this genus of interventionism was the response of this country to the events growing out of the Second World War. It was that conflict that provided the really crucial impetus for a general policy of reaction that would serve to represent the dominant leitmotif of the country's interventionism in the years afterward. Recognizing what it came to view as a major threat to its way of life emanating from Soviet Russia as the fountainhead of a subversive international communist movement, America arrived at the conclusion that it would be obligated to use its material power, political leadership, and moral suasion to dominate and orchestrate the worldwide struggle that developed.

It is this writer's contention, however, that a general American interventionism on behalf of the status quo would in all probability have occurred in any case, although most probably not in as massive a fashion. This belief stems from a conviction that many of the developments of a rapidly transforming world milieu over these years would have required an active American response in terms of its national tradition of foreign policy, most especially on behalf of its historic tendency to champion the values of harmony and consensus in the face of mounting challenges.

We must remember that nowhere is the American identification with the status quo more complete than in the general area of international procedure. Peaceful and orderly change are seen to be crucial for the maintenance of peace in the world. On this point the country has felt it cannot make any concession. To that end, whether it is undertaken by military means, or via the instrumentalities of its economic power, America's interventions have taken the country into virtually every corner of the globe. These interventions have all had one thing in common: a refusal to accept or to adjust to the inevitable violence and radicalism that have tended to mark the processes of change in much of the Third World. It is not only communist revolutions that Americans would come to deplore and actively oppose but revolutions in general.[34]

Over and over again in the post-1945 era—in the Western Hemisphere, in Asia, and in Africa—the nation's very real sympathies for orderly, incremental change would dissolve into hostility when the movements for reform in these countries advocated not only emancipation but "radical" measures designed to fundamentally alter their own situations. And officials in Washington would exhibit virtual panic whenever they discerned evidence that these foreign revolutionary movements were "communist influenced."[35] Thus, once enjoying an overwhelming reputation as a dynamic, progressive, and revolutionary society, America after World War II emerged as the champion *par excellence* of the status quo. While the liberal component, as we have seen, would play a meaningful role in the nation's interventionist posture, it was an overweening desire to protect its privileged position that would lead this country to intervene actively in the world on behalf of a status quo it has continued to view as congenial to its own best interests.

The Interventionist Urge in Perspective

On its face, intervention is neither a sin nor a panacea. It is an approach to dealing with others, and like all techniques it should be directly related to the goals and objectives set forth to realize the national purpose of the country. Otherwise, it is likely to become an end in itself, dragging nations down paths they never intended to follow, toward goals their peoples find repugnant. Unhappily, this has not infrequently been the case with America's approach to intervention.

America's commitment to interventionism, for whatever reason, has reflected a persisting weakness in its foreign policy: a penchant for espousing grandiose principles at the expense of a calm and reasoned assessment of national interest. Too often America's interventions have seemed to be imposed upon it by its emotions rather than by a rational assessment of political realities. This is not so much the fault of the public but of its leaders, who are often tempted to use slogans to justify their actions and then, unwittingly, become prisoners of their own words. The liberal motivation underlying the nation's interventions has certainly reflected this reality.

Looked at historically, one can certainly agree that America's liberal interventionism has from time to time encouraged and fostered the growth and preservation of democratic values in the world, contributing to the development of the idea of equality in freedom. Once can hardly fault the nation for its idealistic attitude in this matter, for its vision of a world made safe for democracy. To the degree that the Monroe Doctrine, for example, was an expression of America's desire in the Western Hemisphere to prevent foreign domination of that region so as to promote the inculcation of democratic systems, it may well have helped to dissuade the European great powers from extending the principle of monarchical rule into the area. There is little doubt, further, that the country's frequent verbal interventions on behalf of its liberal values encouraged and enhanced the development of these concepts elsewhere.

In reacting to the many crisis situations that occurred abroad during America's historical development, it was almost inevitable that whatever it did would constitute some sort of intervention in the domestic lives of other nations. Nationalist patriots everywhere were influenced by America's achievements. For this reason, although the young, "upstart" nation rarely involved itself directly in other countries on behalf of its liberal values during the first century or so of its existence, she was regarded by not a few of the world's major states as a dangerous country.

But measured against any "victories" achieved by America in giving vent to its liberal interventionist inclinations, one must be aware of a number of problems and drawbacks in the orientation. The negative consequences that have ensued from a continuing application of this interventionist mode are sufficiently important to raise fundamental doubts about whether, under all but the most unusual circumstances, America's interventionism on behalf of its democratic values has actually furthered the national purpose of equality in freedom.

First, it must be recognized that the impulse is a narrow, self-centered, and limited approach to foreign affairs, expressive of the nation's special sense of mission in the world. Most of the key assumptions basic to the inclination are attitudes long associated with liberal thought in America: the notion that democracy is a universally valid ideology, the view that the spread of democracy is the equivalent of maintaining international peace and security, and the presumption that underdeveloped societies are bound to move in the direction of political democracy, given the opportunities to do so. But the degree to which non-Western societies adhere to these assumptions is certainly a matter open to dispute.

Second, the parochial derivation of the liberal interventionist impulse runs counter to social and economic realities elsewhere. America's sometimes arrogant assertion that other nations must incorporate its democratic principles, if not copy its own political institutions, frequently serves to confirm in others the ignorance and naîveté of the American people about the conditions necessary to establish and to support democracy in the rest of the world. The evidence seems to be, as we have suggested, that many societies will either acquiesce in or opt for non-democratic arrangements in lieu of democratic ones. The notion that the principle of self-determination will always come out right—that no people, for example, will ever vote itself into "communism"—must be seen in this light. This presumption, in turn, is based on the postulate that no nation ever willingly turns to dictatorship and that to a people intent on national independence, communism anywhere means automatic subordination to an outside government. In America's relationships with others in the post-1945 period, these assumptions were deeply ingrained in our national psyche.

More generally, America's historic periods of intervention have been reflective of a kind of missionary "busybodyness" that makes productive decision-making difficult. To divest itself of its isolationist moods, America has seemed to feel it has to be in command of the situation—whether through unilateral action when others are unwilling to cooperate or, in the post-1945 era, as dominant head of a coalition, exercising the prerogatives of "multilateralizing" its point of view.[36]   When America intervenes, it is with the assurance in the acceptability of its total leadership. This has been the case not only of the country's governments historically but of American business as well.[37]

In responding to the many crises and developments abroad in its history, America has frequently not understood the real-life complexities of those situations in which it has involved itself. Only a well-understood philosophical perspective and an incisive conception of the international system's main currents permit a nation to distinguish those events that require its intervention and those that do not. This is always a challenge for any nation's policy-makers; it is especially difficult for a nation isolated in time. The performance of this country in international affairs in the last half of the twentieth century provides disconcerting evidence of its failure to make those sorts of discriminations.

It is the fundamental dualism of its isolationist-interventionist posture, however, that has posed the greatest dilemmas for the nation in its relationships with other countries—a duopoly to which we now turn in a final assessment of this impulse in the historical mainstream of America's foreign affairs tradition.

THE ISOLATIONIST-INTERVENTIONIST DUOPOLY

As we have endeavored to show, the nature of America's isolationism–interventionism must be seen for what it is: one of the most important, frequently manifested characteristics of America's historic approach to foreign affairs. The chief feature of this dualism is an oscillation once described by Dexter Perkins as phases of withdrawal to phases of dynamic, almost messianic striding upon the world's stage.[38] The shifts between the poles of isolation and intervention represent a preference for extremes in America's relations with others—measures having in common the intention to avoid the contamination of unhealthy foreign troubles. The consistent exhibition of this syndrome in the country's foreign policy-making confirms America's lack of confidence in working constructively with others.[39]

It is well to remember here that those with whom this country has cooperated in its history have not normally been its equals; they have been either dependents, ranging from Latin America after the early 1800s to Britain after World War II, or superiors with whom America has had a number of vexing experiences. While America's dependents have been of various sorts—ranging from subordinates to clients—they have tended to be inferior in terms of capability so as to deny the nation the experience of working with equals. The one time America ended up a partner among equals—1917–1919—the experience was too much to endure. Isolation once again asserted itself as America withdrew to its "continental paradise" across the sea.

Then, too, America's long experience in self-reliance has been interspersed with episodes of global entanglement that, while sometimes effectively managed, have brought enormous disappointment and frustration. These would have been less if the expectations engendered by America's happy past had been more modest. But the world has generally resisted America's zeal in these instances. Hence, America has typically withdrawn once again from the world, not yet having located that happy medium. As in the great reversal of 1920, America's isolationism has had a way of following the frustrations of an overindulgent interventionism. When America's complacency has tended to contribute to crisis, its preference for isolation has tended to breed intervention. Then, too, overcommitment in one part of the world has tended to lead to passivity and abdication of responsibility elsewhere. These habits of action have been marked by the old moral separateness, the belief in the special goodness of America. In this way its isolationism and interventionism are compensatory assertions of independence from the world and a partial repudiation of that world. To that degree, they represent virulent excesses of cultural parochialism.

Nowhere was this problem more consistently demonstrated than in the country's conduct between the two world wars. America's actions during these years highlighted a deep bifurcation in the American mind regarding the proper response to the growing dangers posed by Nazi Germany and Japan. Isolationism was unquestionably the preferred and cherished stance. Yet by the late 1930s, the sentiments of both the American people and their leaders were tilting distinctly in favor of active intervention on behalf of Europe's democracies. This did not prevent the nation from staying out of the struggle almost until the last minute. In retrospect, it is fair to say that the country's policy of nonintervention in Europe and Far Eastern affairs was a disaster—for America and for the cause of democracy. The American nation's record of "too little, too late" contributed to the most destructive war in the history of the world.[40]

Today, the isolationist-interventionist duopoly continues to present the nation with a profound dilemma: The long tradition of American non-involvement in foreign affairs has imparted to the country's diplomacy a certain lack of vision that the post-World War II veering to the extreme of total involvement has not completely overcome. While all of this would not paralyze American foreign policy during these years, it created a permanent tension between the requirements of the external situations in which the nation found itself after 1945 and the country's inner psychological needs and hopes and therefore shaped the mood and the manner in which America picked up the challenge of dealing with Soviet Russia and its allies.

NOTES

1. Quoted in Norman A. Graebner, *Ideas and Diplomacy: Readings in the Intellectual Tradition of American Foreign Policy* (New York: Oxford University Press, 1964), pp. 88–89.

2. Charles Beard, *Giddy Minds and Foreign Quarrels* (New York: Macmillan, 1939), reprinted in Robert A. Goldwin, ed., *Readings in American Foreign Policy*, 2nd ed. (New York: Oxford University Press, 1971), pp. 131–133.

3. Quoted in Norman A. Graebner, "Isolationism," in *International Encyclopedia of the Social Sciences*, 8 (New York: Crowell, Collier and Macmillan, 1968), p. 218.

4. See the elaborate synthesis made by Albert K. Weinberg, "The Historical Meaning of the American Doctrine of Isolation," *American Political Science Review* (June, 1940), pp. 101–148. There is also an excellent commentary on the subject in Cecil V. Crabb, Jr., *Policy-Makers and Critics: Conflicting Theories of American Foreign Policy* (New York: Praeger, 1976), Chapter 1.

5. Support for these observations may be found in numerous public opinion polls taken during the post-1945 era. See also the commentaries on the subject of the following writers: Felix Morley, *The Foreign Policy of the United States* (New York: Alfred A. Knopf, 1951); Gabriel Almond, *The American People and Foreign Policy* (New York: Praeger, 1960); Bernard C. Cohen, *The Public's Impact on Foreign Policy* (Boston: Little, Brown, 1973); Barry B. Hughes, *The Domestic Content of American Foreign Policy* (San Francisco: Freeman, 1978); James N. Rosenau, ed., *Domestic Sources of Foreign Policy* (New York: Free Press, 1967); Robert G. Weissberg, *Public Opinion and Popular Government* (Englewood Cliffs, N.J.:

Prentice-Hall, 1976); and Robert Erikson and Norman Luttbeg, *American Public Opinion* (New York: Wiley, 1973).

6. Thomas A. Bailey, as cited in Sheldon Appleton, *United States Foreign Policy: An Introduction with Cases* (Boston: Little, Brown, 1968), p. 39, makes this point.

7. On this point, see Frederick H. Hartmann, *The New Age of American Foreign Policy* (New York: Macmillan, 1970), pp. 26-37.

8. Cited in Arthur E. Ekirch, Jr., *Ideas, Ideals and American Diplomacy* (New York: Appleton-Century-Crofts, 1966), p. 103.

9. Crabb, *Policy-Makers and Critics*, p. 20, makes this case.

10. See Edward Vose Gulick, *Europe's Classical Balance of Power* (Ithaca, N.Y.: Cornell University Press, 1955); and Henry Kissinger, *A World Restored: Metternich, Castlereagh, and the Problem of Peace* (Boston: Houghton-Mifflin, 1957). See, also, his more recent *Diplomacy* (New York: Simon & Schuster, 1994), esp. Chapters 3–6.

11. Crabb, *Policy-Makers and Critics* , p. 23.

12. See Almond, *The American People*; Weissberg, *Public Opinion*, p. 34; and Don D. Smith, "Dark Areas of Ignorance Revisited," in Don D. Nimmo and Charles Bonjean, eds., *Political Attitudes and Public Opinion* (New York: McKay, 1972), pp. 267–272.

13. The sentiments expressed by the presidential campaign of Patrick Buchanan in 1996 are reflective of this view.

14. Crabb, *Policy-Makers and Critics,* p. 35.

15. For a useful overview of the record of America's interventionism down into the Eisenhower administration, see Doris A. Graber, *Crisis Diplomacy: A History of U.S. Intervention Policies and Practices* (Washington, D.C.: Public Affairs Press, 1959). George Washington, in his last days, pointed to the problems inherent in America undertaking such a role. In his Farewell Address (September 18, 1796), Washington cautioned his fellow citizens against "permanent, inveterate antipathies against particular nations" (for example, Britain) and "passionate attachments for others" (for example France)—a warning issued to counteract what he saw even then as an urge among some Americans to intervene abroad on behalf of freedom and democracy.

16. Quoted in Claude Julien, *America's Empire* (New York: Random House, 1973), p. 11.

17. William Appleman Williams, *America Confronts a Revolutionary World* (New York: William Morrow, 1976), p. 42.

18. A number of revisionist historians in this country have pointed to expansionism as a major root cause of the difficulties faced by America in the post-1945 world. In a general sense, Max Lerner has cited the expansionist urge as underlying the country's foreign policies as a superpower. William Appleman Williams argues that a commitment to a worldwide Open Door Policy fueled the country's globalism after World War II. The basic aim of the globalist Open Door principle, for Williams, was to obtain and manipulate unlimited access to the world's economic markets in order to preserve prosperity and hence order at home. Richard J. Barnet has argued that America's expansionism amounted to a policy of acquiring an ever-increasing dominion over other people. For him, however, the nation's historic territorial acquisitions account for only a portion of America's expansionist history. Lerner's position may be seen in *America as a Civilization* (New York: Simon &

Schuster, 1957). Williams views are set forth in his *The Tragedy of American Diplomacy* (Chicago: Rand McNally, 1956); those of Barnet in *Roots of War: The Men and Institutions behind U.S. Foreign Policy* (New York: Atheneum, 1972) and with Ronald Mueller in *Global Reach: The Power of the Multinational Corporation* (New York: Simon & Schuster, 1974). See also Gabriel Kolko, *The Roots of American Foreign Policy* (Boston: Beacon Press, 1969).

19. Included in that total, of course, was Alaska, which, by itself, incorporates over 580,000 square miles.

20. Witness the policy of Theodore Roosevelt in Panama vis-à-vis Colombia at the turn of the century. The annexation of the Philippines also comes to mind in this regard. American troops were sent to suppress the rebellion of native Filipinos, which broke out almost immediately after the American victory over the Spanish. The resulting pacification effort lasted nearly ten years at a substantial loss of life.

21. Cited in Ruhl J. Bartlett, *The Record of American Diplomacy*, 4th ed. (New York: Alfred A. Knopf, 1964), p. 385.

22. On the notion of destiny built into the American experience, see Anders Stephanson, *Manifest Destiny: American Expansion and the Empire of Right* (New York: Hill and Wang, 1995).

23. Among the more stimulating works dealing with this period of American expansion, culminating with the Mexican War, are Norman A. Graebner, *Empire on the Pacific: A Study in American Continental Expansion* (New York: Ronald Press, 1955); and Frederick Merk, *Manifest Destiny and Mission in American History: A Reinterpretation* (New York: Alfred A. Knopf, 1963). See also his *The Monroe Doctrine and American Expansionism, 1843–1849* (New York: Alfred A. Knopf, 1966); and David M. Pletcher, *The Diplomacy of Annexation: Texas, Oregon, and the Mexican War* (Columbia: University of Missouri Press, 1973).

24. *Foreign Relations of the United States* (FRUS), 1, *1895* (Washington, D.C.: Government Printing Office, 1896), p. 558.

25. This period is treated well in the following works: Walter LaFeber, *The New Empire: An Interpretation of American Expansion, 1860–1898* (Ithaca, N.Y.: Cornell University Press, 1963); David Healy, *United States Expansionism: The Imperialist Urge in the 1890s* (Madison: University of Wisconsin Press, 1970); and H. Wayne Morgan, *America's Road to Empire: The War with Spain and Overseas Expansion* (New York: Wiley, 1965). An older, oft-cited work is Julius W. Pratt's *Expansionists of 1898* (Baltimore, Md.: Johns Hopkins University Press, 1936). For a general introduction to the entire period, see Ernest R. May, *Imperial Democracy: The Emergence of America as a Great Power* (New York: Harcourt, Brace, Jovanovich, 1961).

26. The "Open Door" toward China, William Howard Taft's "dollar diplomacy" in the Caribbean and Central America, and the general tendency of Presidents Wilson, Harding, and Coolidge to orchestrate the affairs of America's neighbors to the south represent the major illustrations of this tendency.

27. The Monroe Doctrine is, and remains, a phrase with which most attentive Americans are familiar, and the package of emotional reactions that it evokes has had a powerful impact on the actual policy of America. This story is well told in Dexter Perkins, *Hands Off: A History of the Monroe Doctrine* (Boston: Little, Brown and Company, 1941); and in Samuel Flagg Bemis, *The Latin American Policy of the United States* (New York: Harcourt, Brace & World, 1943).

28. On this point, see Charles O. Lerche, Jr., *Foreign Policy of the American People*, 3rd ed. (Englewood Cliffs, N.J.: Prentice-Hall, 1967), p. 113. For a general discussion of the tendency of all empires in history to justify their actions in terms of a "higher calling," see J. A. Hobson, *Imperialism: A Study*, 3rd ed. (London: George Allen and Unwin, 1938), esp. pp. 196–198.

29. Most of the beliefs and values inherent in "the American way of life"—freedom, equality, democracy, progress, the potential for human betterment, faith in rational processes, and the scientific method—are principles of the "liberal political faith." To the liberal mind, freedom is essential for the full actualization of the human spirit; freedom and democracy are also inseparable. Two ideas of the traditional liberal mentality have had direct relevance for foreign affairs: a belief that human society is, or can be, harmonious and cooperative, and a faith in the inevitability of growth and progress.

30. Robert Palmer notes, *Age of the Democratic Revolution, 1760–1800*, Vol. 1, *The Challenge* (Princeton, N. J.: Princeton University Press, 1959), p. 241: "In Ireland and in the Dutch provinces, they [the sympathizers with the Americans] formed militia companies, wore uniforms, attended drills and built up an actual revolutionary pressure."

31. Indeed, the Italian struggle for freedom was led by the patriot Guiseppe Mazzini (1805–1872), who called for America to act as a "nation-guide" for the democratic forces of Europe. For the American response to the Greek independence movement, see Theodore Saloutos, *The Greeks in the United States* (Cambridge, Mass.: Harvard University Press, 1964); and Stephen A. Larrabee, *Hellas Observed: The American Experience of Greece, 1775–1865* (New York: New York University Press, 1957). For the appeal to America of the Polish plight during these years, see Jerzy Jan Lerski, *A Polish Chapter in Jacksonian America: The United States and the Polish Exiles of 1831* (Madison: University of Wisconsin Press, 1958). For the impact of the 1848 upheavals on Americans, see Carl Wittke, *Refugees of Revolution: The German Forty-Eighters in America* (Philadelphia: University of Pennsylvania Press, 1952). For the country's reaction to the Hungarian revolt, see Emil Lengyel, *Americans from Hungary* (Philadelphia: Lippincott, 1948); and John G. Gazley, *American Opinion of German Unification, 1848–1871* (New York: Columbia University Press, 1926). See also Graebner, *Ideas and Diplomacy*, esp. pp. 309–310.

32. Useful treatments of Sino-American relations during this period are Foster Rhea Dulles, *China and America: The Story of Their Relations Since 1784* (Princeton, N.J.: Princeton University Press, 1946); John K. Fairbank, *The United States and China,* rev. ed. (New York: Viking Press, 1948); and Warren I. Cohen, *America's Response to China: An Interpretive History of Sino-American Relations* (New York: Wiley, 1971).

During the years 1910–1911 in Mexico a liberal democratic movement led by Francisco Madero succeeded in overthrowing the long (1876–1910) Porfirio Diaz dictatorship. America had high hopes for it, but in 1913 it too was overthrown in a brutal military golpe ushering in the despotic Huerta regime. Wilson, referring to the Huerta clique as a "government of butchers," became compulsively determined to depose Huerta and, in his words, teach Latin Americans "to elect good men." Armed military intervention occurred in both 1914 (the "Vera Cruz crisis") and later in 1917 when General John Pershing was sent into the country at the head of a force of some 7,000 men to hunt down the "bandit chieftan" Pancho Villa.

Useful overviews of American policy toward Mexico during this period may be found in Howard F. Cline, *The United States and Mexico* (Cambridge, Mass.: Harvard University Press, 1953); Charles W. Hackett, *The Mexican Revolution and the United States, 1910–1926* (Boston: World Peace Foundation, 1926). Two analyses centering on Wilson's approach are Harley Notter, *The Origins of the Foreign Policy of Woodrow Wilson* (Baltimore: Johns Hopkins University Press, 1937), and Robert E. Quirk, *An Affair of Honor: Woodrow Wilson and the Occupation of Veracruz* (Lexington: University of Kentucky Press, 1962).

33. Beginning in the 1920s and extending over many decades down to the present time, America agreed voluntarily to impose limitations on the exercise of its growing national power in relation to Latin America. Gradually, Washington's interventionist inclination gave way to the sharing with the Latin American states of responsibility for both decision and action in important areas of inter-American affairs, particularly in the maintenance of peace and security. Yet, despite these improvements in the relationship between America and its neighbors to the south, the country has continued to exercise its "sovereign right" to engage in interventions in the name of its national interest.

One of the best accounts of the developing inter-American impulse for cooperation, sometimes at the expense of America's interventionist tendencies, remains J. Lloyd Mecham, *The United States and Inter-American Security, 1889–1960* (Austin: University of Texas Press, 1961).

34. See, in this vein, Stephen E. Ambrose, *Rise to Globalism: American Foreign Policy since 1938,* 8th, rev. ed. (Baltimore: Penguin Books, 1997); Gabriel Kolko in William Taubman, ed., *Globalism and Its Critics: The American Foreign Policy Debate of the 1960s* (Lexington, Mass.: D. C. Heath, 1973); Bernard S. Morris, *International Communism and American Foreign Policy* (New York: Atherton Press, 1966); Ronald Steel, *Pax Americana* (New York: Viking Press, 1970); J. William Fulbright, *The Arrogance of Power* (New York: Random House, 1966); Neil Houghton's "Foreword" in his *Struggle against History: U.S. Foreign Policy in an Age of Revolution* (New York: Simon & Schuster, 1968); and Richard Walton, *Cold War and Counter-Revolution: The Foreign Policy of John F. Kennedy* (Baltimore: Penguin Books, 1972).

35. This is not to say, of course, that America did not accommodate Communist Party–state regimes from time to time when it felt it to be in its national interest to do so. Nevertheless, these accommodations, whether they be Yugoslavia after 1948 or the Peoples Republic of China from the early 1970s, must be seen in the broader context of America's self-proclaimed struggle with Soviet Russia.

36. The American-led coalition that assaulted Iraq in early 1991 is a case in point.

37. American business has been inclined to be unsharing in its own fashion: in its investment priorities, in the organization of management, in its attitude toward local social mores and procedures, and in the distribution of benefits. Richard Barnet is particularly eloquent on this point. See his *Roots of War*, esp. Part II: "The Political Economy of Expansionism."

38. See Dexter Perkins, *The American Approach to Foreign Policy* (Cambridge, Mass.: Harvard University Press, 1952), esp. Chapter 7.

39. It is a virtual truism that Americans become political isolationists when they cannot dominate international affairs and internationalists when they can.

40. For American policy beginning with Roosevelt's "quarantine" speech

in October 1937 and leading up to the nation's entry into the war, see Robert A. Divine, *The Illusion of Neutrality* (Chicago: University of Chicago Press, 1962). Still valuable are the two volumes by William L. Langer and S. Everett Gleason, *The Challenge of Isolation* (New York: Harper & Row, 1952), and *The Undeclared War* (New York: Harper & Row, 1953).

CHAPTER 5

Tradition Manifest: The American Concept of Alliance

The charming feature of international politics is that no one need ever grow tired of friends and enemies. Wait a short time; they will have changed places.
—Nicholas Spykman

Toward the end of the Second World War, America found itself in a virtually unique position in world history. Blessed by a bountiful fate with unparalleled material resources and human energies, the country was faced with an international situation that seemingly afforded it ample opportunity to translate these advantages into benefits not only for its own people but for the rest of mankind. But the American people were not able, as it turned out, to effect the sort of humane and constructive relationship with the rest of the world that one would have hoped.

In the last months of the war, America moved ahead confidently with plans to ensure that its citizens would have a more stable and amenable environment in which to prosper—a belief predicated in large part on an effective application of the principles of the Atlantic Charter, institutionalized in the structure of the new United Nations Organization. Within three years, these hopes lay floundering under the weight of an alarming, rapidly intensifying conflict with Soviet Russia. The Russian-American Cold War confrontation had dawned and would soon be translated into a struggle played out on many stages, plunging innumerable peoples into miasmas of death and destruction in a process that would last for some forty years.

A consensus quickly developed in this country concerning the root cause of this state of affairs: the perceived threat of Russian-inspired "communist" aggression and subversion. America's foreign policies were improvised in the late 1940s and early 1950s by people who were convinced that the one real danger to universal peace and tranquility was constituted by a worldwide communist conspiracy. It was to this threat—believed to have been maintained, in one fashion or another, at a constant threshold of danger—that much of America's foreign policy after 1945 was directed.

Throughout the Cold War era, America's basic orientation remained constant. Insofar as Soviet Russia and its friends were responsible for the constant exacerbation of international tensions, for the failure of the United Nations to keep the peace, and for the continuing threat of general war, America's vigilance had to be kept at a high level so that its necessarily extensive involvement in world affairs could be successfully carried forward. Only in this fashion would the fundamental values of the American people have a realistic chance of survival in an ever-dangerous international system.

Unfortunately, Americans were just not psychologically prepared during and after that conflict to assume the burdens of world responsibility. It seems as if history itself decided to play some sort of monstrous joke upon us. At the very moment when the nation stepped squarely onto the world stage, the nature of that arena underwent a rather drastic change. The very makeup of the international system became rather remote from its former reality, as the bipolar era came to pass.

Predictably, America, rushing backwards into the future, sought to adapt the older classical diplomatic and political approaches, with which it had always been uncomfortable and with which it never really had had much experience, to meet its new international challenges. But the older order had passed, and consequently, Americans had to try to internalize, simultaneously and in a hurry, those tested qualities of traditional diplomatic wisdom that were still valuable, such as the need for moderation and flexibility in dealing with others, and those thorny new techniques of statecraft that virtually no one knew, such as the proper role for foreign aid, the development of an effective use of propaganda, and the conduct of the new warfare. In addition, the suddenness with which America assumed world leadership added difficulty to a situation already challenging enough.

Nowhere were these difficulties more evidenced than in the country's approach to alliances, for it would be in America's conception and practice of alliances that its tradition of foreign affairs would most clearly be manifested with all its contradictions and flaws. Once the decision to confront Soviet Russia with all the intensity at America's disposal had been made, it only remained to take the necessary steps to put teeth into it. Rather astonishingly, given the country's historic disdain for permanent commitment, it would prove to be the time-tested alliance vehicle that would come in the fullness of time to serve as America's chief line of defense in a boiling sea of troubles—a political vehicle that America had always rejected throughout its peacetime history in the name of a self-righteous and moralistic national unilateralism.

THE PSYCHOLOGICAL MOOD

As the image began to crystallize in Washington at the end of the Second World War that Moscow was taking a dichotomous view of the world as divided into communist and non-communist camps, America's decision-makers felt obliged to counteract this blatant assumption. They did so by attempting to turn Russian logic on itself. Accepting the dichotomy, on Moscow's terms, Washington merely modified one of the rules: The world was henceforth to be communist or anti-communist and that was that. Moscow's leadership of a monolithic sector of the globe was now to be countered by Washington's control of an equally united but hopefully stronger aggregation. Thus, the notion of the "free world" was given flesh. That Washington should now turn to the alliance was certainly surprising, given its traditional orientation, but what was most astonishing was that America proceeded to employ the alliance with a single-minded determination virtually unprecedented in the annals of the nation-state system.[1]

But while accepting the alliance rationale as a viable policy technique for the enhancement of its security in the postwar world, America proceeded to go about the business of employing the old classical vehicle in a manner that complicated rather than facilitated whatever chances may have existed for the achievement of a mutually satisfying settlement with the Russians. Furthermore, America's rather novel concept of the nature and function of alliances, by unnecessarily alienating a number of other states (both those who participated in these alliances and those who did not), would contribute in due course to an undermining of the very stability of many of those areas that the policy was designed to insure.

To analyze, then, the fabric of America's alliance rationale in the years after the Second World War is to drive to the very heart of one of the most persistently exhibited weaknesses in the country's relationship with the rest of the world: an inability to separate the facts of international life from what we Americans would like those realities to be.

THE STRATEGIC FRAMEWORK

Every policy-maker, of necessity, is presented with the task of deciding at a given time upon the national interest. That interest is a confluence of numerous factors, including geography, environmental conditioning, cultural values, economic imperatives, and not least, the nation's psychological makeup. In conceptualizing the relationship of these factors to the national purpose, the policy-maker usually turns to history.

Two classic definitions of national interest are clear and unambiguous. One—perhaps the only one not capable of a depressing number of alternatives—is the primordial interest of self-preservation, that which William Pitt once called the "first law of nature" for a sovereign state. There is in addition the geographical factor—national interest being interpreted as an expression of a country's location in space as an obvious element of strategy. America, in fact, was for a time able to define its prime national interest in geographical terms centering around its role as an important hemispheric state. But in the world of the 1940s that interest had already begun to recede into a place of lesser prominence, as merely one among a host of other more complex and diffuse interests.

Beyond self-preservation and geography the national interest becomes rather elusive. Unhappily, it became fashionable for American policy-makers in the early postwar era to define the national interest in the highly generalized terms of "Peace," "Security," "Freedom," "Justice," "Well-Being," and "Prosperity." So defined, the term did not tell the American decision-maker, for example, how to act toward Soviet Russia in a given situational context, nor whether rearmament posed a greater danger to American security than disarmament, nor what kind of objectives the country should be striving for in its relationships with particular countries in Asia, Africa, and Latin America.

That the national interest was in fact thought of in this manner at all may be better understood if one remembers that in the late 1940s American foreign policy decision-makers were faced with a tradition that they deemed far from enviable. It was time, we were told, for America to "grow up" and abandon such utopian "inanities" as "unconditional surrender," the Paris Peace Pact of 1928, and the sort of destructive moralist exercises epitomized by the Stimson Doctrine. America's initial postwar foreign policy orientation thus developed, at least superficially, in a milieu of reaction to the old "liberal-utopian" approach to world affairs that had been paramount in American dealings with the world in the 1920s and 1930s.

The most crucial event in this respect was the development and formulation of the policy of containment. *As an operational approach*, whatever its initial content or later alterations, containment originally reflected a desire by America to accept the traditional role of a great state in the international realm. To this extent the doctrine cannot be faulted. At least two elements of this policy marked a self-conscious and welcome break with the utopian idealism of the nation's past: the assumption of world wide American interests and the willingness to employ force, if required, to maintain those interests.

Once having taken this basic departure from historic practice, however, it was particularly vital how succeeding cadres of American decision-making elite would view the international system (and regional sub-systems) in which the new approach was to be implemented. An examination of the record of the next half century reveals that a peculiarly refractory American image of the world, rather than a realistic appraisal of the facts of international political life, tended to dominate the foreign policy-making process in Washington.

As a result of a belated but no less genuine perception of Soviet Russia as a threat to the security of the American nation, combined with an acceptance of the reality of having to live in an uncertain and unpredictable world, a very powerful internal consensus quickly developed as to the proper thrust of American alliance policy. Nothing was more indicative of this newly found consensus than the characterization at this time of Russian-American relations as a "Cold War." And it was not long before the idea of the Cold War came to transform the traditional state concern for the ordering of national goals, and the instrumentation of power to that end, into a more comprehensive, omnipresent, and total struggle for ever more and more power as the central tenet of the new American image. In a word, American foreign policy decision-makers allowed themselves during those crucial years to entertain the simple belief that once they had properly ascertained the real source of all the difficulty and moved to counteract it, that would be all that there was to it. There was no point in attempting to deal with the communist threat by dissipating it or diverting it; only direct opposition could halt it, and only local, and ultimately general, superiority of strength could turn it back.

The history and national character of the American people aided in the manner in which the conflict would be waged. War, even a Cold War, in America's foreign affairs tradition, has always been a much simpler exercise than peace, since the goal in warfare—victory—is intrinsic to the task and permits no major modification. All else becomes a matter of tactics, a problem of deciding how best to win the victory that is so important as not to require definition.[2]

THE RATIONALE

America's alliance policy came into being piecemeal in differing circumstances but designed to fulfill essentially the same functions.[3] Taken as a totality, it would serve two broad concepts that American public opinion, at least until the latter phases of the country's involvement in Vietnam, assumed to be compatible. The first was that the "free world" was a recognizable entity; that its principal concerns were military protection and political vigilance against "communist" aggression and subversion; that the primary object of its external relations was the geographic containment of Soviet Russia and its followers. The second concept was that, American interests being world wide in scope, it would be advantageous for their retention that it should appear in virtually every situation, either directly or by proxy, as an international strategic factor with which to be reckoned.

The Operational Credo

Once America came to regard the forces of international communism as the primary adversary to be confronted on the world stage, it was felt that there could be no equivocation in its efforts to restrain the vicious monolith. The entire noncommunist world would become the arena of American action. Not all parts of this enormous area were to be of equal priority, however; some regions were immediately important because of their relatively greater susceptibility to Russian bloc pressure, others because of the greater contribution they could make to the common effort, and still others because of their local significance. The great variety in internal and regional conditions, furthermore, made the development of a single system and organization of containment exceptionally difficult and unlikely. In this way, America came to the regional approach as permitting the necessary variation in timing, commitment, organizational detail, and operational planning from one particular region to another.

The regional approach was preferrable for a number of reasons. To begin with, regional arrangements made it possible for America to express its worldwide interests through cooperative efforts. In this way, American national interests could be extended throughout every region of the globe by means of a consensus of the local states involved. Furthermore, by submerging its own interests in regional organizations, America's policies might not appear to others to be so self-serving.

Second, Washington believed Moscow had to be convinced that we meant business. "Mere" bilateral arrangements with individual countries could easily be broken or used as pawns in negotiating important agreements, but the publicly pledged word of regional alliance commitments would be much more persuasive to Soviet Russia's leaders. Thus, Washington evidently believed that the Russian government would be more persuaded of the intensity of the American commitment if its alliance arrangements were made on a regional basis.[4]

Third, convinced that it was now the military, political, and economic leader of the free world, America felt morally obligated to protect its allies against the likelihood of communist aggression. For the sake of convenience, American protection could be more effectively dispensed through broad regional organizations, rather than by means of arrangements on a seriatim basis. In this way, America could not be accused of favoritism, a charge that might be leveled at American foreign policy if bilateral arrangements were made the basis for its alliances.

Finally, it was discovered that the regional approach might well have a great advantage in the context of the newly formed United Nations Organization. Thus it was America that insisted in the dialogue leading up to and including the San Francisco Conference in early summer 1945 that some sort of clause be incorporated into the Charter permitting the creation of regional security arrangements. Article 51 was then elaborated, which allowed for collective self-defense through regional organizations to be created outside of the UN system but within the principles of the Charter. In this way, regional collective security efforts would escape the Russian veto in the Security Council, and America could pursue its own course without interference from Moscow.[5]

As America's Cold War posture was extended from the original 1947 Rio de Janeiro Treaty initiative into Europe via the North Atlantic Treaty Organization (NATO) and, then, in the 1950s, into the larger international arena, the ongoing American orientation was to replicate a series of alliances on the basis of a model prototype treaty. These alliances became the vehicles for an involvement that would entail not only our political advice and aid in military organization and strategy but also our oversight in the employment of police, the use of domestic propaganda and indoctrination, the extension of economic assistance, and the methodology of finance and trade.

In the process, American decision-makers inevitably had to deal with a number of ticklish questions: What sort of allies should we seek? What importance should be attached to the internal political systems of the members? Operationally, which should have higher priority within the overall alliance rationale: rapid buildup of allied military capability or the development of stable regimes with long-term survival value? Finally, to what extent should the hegemonic implications of America's role in these regional arrangements be openly faced? In the years after the process was begun, the administration of America's various alliances would habitually require answers to these questions in immediate terms and specific circumstances—often disparate in nature. Yet, from the record, one can perceive some common denominators in the working of the American theory and practice of alliance.

The Total Appproach. First, these alliances associated America with local (and sometimes other) signatory states in the defense of delimited geographic areas as well as in the regulation of relationships among the state members in specific regions of the globe.

Second, they defined the threat against which the alliance was directed in terms usually vague enough to provide flexibility (and on occasion to avoid provocation as well) but also sufficiently specific as to make it difficult for a member to avoid honoring his promises.

Third, the military aspect of the alliances was allowed to dictate America's practical approach to them. The first requirement, and usually the key one, for a state to qualify as an American ally was for it to accept the military and collective-defense implications of any arrangements made. In practice, this meant that the potential ally be amenable to American military doctrine, to American military aid, and to American military leadership and that it be content to fit the bulk of its own military program into an American-inspired plan.

Fourth, the test as to whether a country would make a good ally for America was essentially an ideological one: Did it have a deep and articulate hostility to communism? With the various regional configurations focusing, as we insisted they do, on the development of military capability and political militancy, any development within an alliance that threatened these qualities was not welcome in Washington. Short-term or immediate military advantage was typically thought of as being more crucial (acceptable) to America than long-range internal stability in an ally; this is why we never particularly cared much whether our allies were parliamentary democracies or military dictatorships, so long as they yelled their anti-communism loudly enough. An important corollary of this view was that each regional bloc was left largely alone to develop and apply a single, unified approach to problems arising in its own area of application. Thus, a supra-military dimension was added to the limited defense engagement as something resembling a bloc was expected to emerge from a particular treaty arrangement.

Fifth, America generally expected a common front from its allies, this uniform posture to show up in at least two ways. On the one hand, on all direct Cold War confrontations, it was envisaged that each regional security organization construct and exemplify a single policy line toward the communist danger. Historically, this led us to seek a common NATO position on Berlin, a solid Organization of American States (OAS) point of view on Cuba, a consensus in the Southeast Asia Treaty Organization (SEATO) on Vietnam, and so on. In addition, American practice tended to count each member of a regional alliance as a "specific" Cold War ally, at the same time trusting in the support of virtually all its allies in problem-solving prosecuted in the broad arena of the United Nations.

Sixth, they all provided for a significant measure of continuing consultation among the members as to the progress of the alliance and for emergency consultation in the event of a perceived threat calling for the invocation of the joint-action provisions of the agreement.

Finally, each was to a lesser or great extent institutionalized by the creation of instruments of multilateral consultation, planning, and action in the military, political, and even socioeconomic fields.

Flowing from this conceptualization of alliance, major problems posing serious dilemmas would arise, a number of which themselves became crises in the postwar period. These realities merit closer consideration and are vital to an understanding of the impact of American alliance policy upon the country's ability to manage well the inevitable conflicts arising out of its broader international relationships, most especially that with Russia both before and after 1991.

A CRITIQUE

A rather sterile, uniform view of its alliance commitments over the years hindered rather than promoted the chances for realistic adjustments of America's relationships with adversary, friend and neutral alike. The difficulty in adopting a more rational approach to America's alliance obligations was that it would put in question the "free world" interventionist tenets a majority of the electorate long accepted and on which the broad conduct of American foreign policy after World War II depended. It is in this sense that, quite apart from the adverse domestic political, economic, and social fallout the Vietnam War engendered, the American role in Southeast Asia served to put into bold relief many of the underlying contradictions and liabilities that marked the general conduct of American foreign policy during much of the post-1945 period.

One conclusion that may be drawn from the difficulties in which

America found itself throughout the post-1945 world is that in its preoccupation with the requirements of containment, reinforced by an oversimple analogy we liked to draw between the task of restraining Soviet Russia and the earlier one of confronting fascism, our leaders tended to ignore the fact that countervailing military and political power projected abroad by formal commitments to protect territorial boundary lines was only one factor, and a problematic one at that, among a host of non-military desiderata that accounted for the deterrence of aggression and subversion in the world of the last half of the twentieth century. Indeed, a number of pathologies afflicted America's approach to alliances from the very beginning.

First, our alliance policy reflected from the outset an acute, almost emotional preoccupation with the power factor in international politics. It was an obsession that mirrored the country's long-standing views on the subject. Whatever else the Cold War mentality generated in Washington, it most surely contributed to the inculcation of the notion of omnipresent and total struggle for ever more power as the central proposition of the new postwar American world view. Unfortunately, what this tended to mean in practice was that the Russian-American conflict was in essence stripped of diplomatic content and simply seen as a test of power.

Such a construct simplified the "intellectual problem" facing the American government. Strategy in the grand sense became more and more superfluous for America's decision-makers as the operational problem of American Cold War policy was reduced to the tactical necessity of opposing any Russian move and, if possible, frustrating it. Indeed, the subsequent abandonment of healthy accommodation and maneuver in America's relationships with both Soviet Russia and the People's Republic of China was clearly signaled by the semantics of the conflict.

Simultaneously, and in the most ironic of fashions, America sought to project its alliance commitments by means of its traditional distrust of Europe's historical experience, most notably the balance of power. This distrust was still strong enough after 1945 that it spurred the policy-makers of the Truman administration to defend the creation of the North Atlantic Treaty before the Congress by explicitly abjuring balance of power semantics.[6] The tendency after 1945 to paint "newer" collective security colors on America's alliances revealed the same residue of suspicion.[7]

Second, America's alliance rationale rested upon a view of commitment at odds both with the requirements of political realism and, frequently, with the interests of its allied states. It would soon be quite apparent that America and many of its alliance partners not only often differed in their understanding of goals and priorities concerning particular alliance commitments but also diverged in the assumptions they made about the intrinsic significance of the act of commitment itself.

The primary difficulty is that Washington did not opt to view its commitments as situational in character. Situational commitment is an approach that focuses on the rationality of particularized courses of action in the context of the requirements of the situation in which a state finds itself. This view of commitment holds that it is inherent in the situation itself, that its verbalization is essentially unimportant, and its realization dependent upon whether it continues to serve the national interest at the time.

America tended, on the other hand, from the moment the ink was dry on the Rio Treaty, to view its alliance commitments as non-situational—a view that stresses that it is useful to retain these arrangements in order to serve, ultimately, interests outside the local context in which the alliance was supposed to apply. The major rationale underlying this view of commitment is that a government must always keep its promises; that once a verbal commitment has been issued, for example, to contain communism, this endeavor should take on a life of its own becoming, in effect, a binding permanent pledge. When the satisfaction of a commitment as a demonstration of resolve or of principle assumes more importance than the appropriateness of the proposed line of action in terms of the interests presumed to structure the original undertaking, the commitment may be said to be non-situational.[8]

It is this conception of commitment that underlay the type of collective security system preferred by Washington after the Second World War. For America, "collective security" came to involve unwavering respect for the moral and legal duty to regard an attack by any state on a member of the designated defense area as an attack on all. To this end, states were expected to fulfill their commitment to collective security not so much because they might have specific interests in the situation at hand as they all were presumed to have a long-range interest in making collective security workable.

The bankruptcy of this view would be demonstrated at many different points in time throughout the Cold War period. One difficulty was how to galvanize states against a threat that they refused to recognize as real. An effort in the mid-1950s by Secretary Dulles to erect an anti-Russian alliance in the Middle East, based primarily on the Arab states, is a case in point. The Baghdad Pact fiasco illustrates clearly how self-defeating it is to arm states against a danger the existence of which they at the very least subordinate to other concerns, especially when such states have unresolved disputes with neighbors. So, too, the American initiative over many years to arm Pakistan against a Chinese state that it had some difficulty in viewing as a threatening entity.

On more than one occasion, an ally of America refused to "honor" its obligations, as Washington viewed them, to the everlasting frustration of its decision makers. The failure of America's major allies to come to its assistance in Southeast Asia was perhaps the most graphic illustration of these basic flaws but was by no means unique.[9] Another reason for the confusion among America's allies in interpreting their mutual alliance commitments was the great problem in defining aggression. This problem stemmed from the difficulty in distinguishing between the factual realities of aggression and the legal labels employed by states to justify actions taken by themselves or to condemn similar actions by others. The concept of aggression is itself a legal conclusion about the nature of a particular pattern of coercion, yet the conceptualization of "aggression" or "armed attack" is so vague that, operationally, states have been left largely alone to determine its content.[10]

Third, America's grasp of alliance amounted to a frequent replication of policy—the quantification syndrome writ large. As the original sense of the classical containment policy defined by Kennan came to be applied elsewhere, it began to be distorted as attention shifted from what had been very largely a European confrontation to a struggle with communism on a worldwide basis. The Baghdad Pact, SEATO, the agreements with Australia and New Zealand (ANZUS), the treaties with Japan and Taiwan, the unilateral American guarantees to Laos and South Vietnam—all repeated the Truman Doctrine's pattern of American military guarantees to threatened states, but under wholly new conditions. The attempts to establish joint staffs on the NATO pattern were carried forward, although without allocated troops. Each of our later alliances were accompanied by an aid program intended to build up the logistical infrastructure of the alliance. The whole process took on a quality of automism: We had a patented policy, applicable to any situation. We came to imagine that this technique of alliance with its military guarantees was appropriate to secure any state—however small and unstable—from communist-sponsored subversion or even from internally generated civil war and communal turmoil.

Fourth, our alliance ethos reflected in many ways the most retrograde elements of the moralist strain of the Puritan Ethic, with its deeply ingrained distrust of outsiders and cultural self-image of uniqueness. After all, we were faced suddenly after the Second World War with something entirely alien to our national experience—the necessity of dealing with allies on a long-haul peacetime basis. Such relationships were bound to be different from our wartime associations where the requirements of the military situation and mutual interdependence had served to lessen friction. Few other countries have ever been more poorly prepared for the give-and-take of coalition diplomacy than America. The strains and stresses our alliances generated over time help explain the mood of resurgent unilateralism among the American people in the 1980s and 1990s.

Certain ingrained prejudices made it difficult for us to accept allies on an equal basis or to understand the peculiar problems that shaped foreign diplomacy. The idea of Old World Machiavellianism, deeply ingrained in the American psyche for so long, was difficult to eradicate. The decision by the French and British, for example, in concert with Israel, to attack Nasser's Egypt in the fall of 1956 without consulting Washington was viewed by the Eisenhower administration in a most outraged of fashions. This condescension was particularly marked in our attitude toward non Western peoples. In this, we demonstrated an insensitivity to some elementary facts: Our own land had been peculiarly blessed by chance with material bounty and geographical advantages that had trickled down to the masses in sufficient measure to moderate class conflict; our general well-being had created a reasonably unified national community; and our economic success had made us notable enthusiasts of the system of free enterprise. Naturally, we were all too prone to take the measure of others by our own experience.

There was little confidence in the intelligence and good intentions of foreigners, and the belief was widespread that other nations would do well to regard us as their mentor. Throughout the period of the great nineteenth century folk migrations, the highest compliment that could be paid to an immigrant was that he had become "Americanized." After World War II, the fourth generation descendents of these uprooted peoples had now achieved comfortable middle class status. Many of them experienced an inward gratification from vaunting their Americanism by deriding foreign nations. Hence the prevailing attitude toward the foibles of our "free world" partners was not a particularly tolerant one. The situation was complicated by the fact that America had to grubstake the proud states of Western Europe before they could become productive allies. There was bound to be a patronizing attitude on the part of Americans that produced a resentment and seeming ingratitude on the part of the peoples who partook of our bounty. Over time, the French came to be particularly resented in this context.

Fifth, America's alliance posture would come to be both a contributing factor to, and a reflection of, a persistent inability to understand any point of view dissenting from the perception of our relationship with Soviet Russia as the primary locus of international affairs. It would be this type of thinking that would contribute so much to making the Third World an unstable and even hostile environment for American interests. Almost from the moment of their creation, the regional alliance blocs diverged in direction. Yet there would be no escape from the logic of America's alliance rationale: If we were serious in our efforts to contain Russian power, each area into which Soviet Russia could be expected to expand had to be kept at a high level of readiness to repel any initiative from Moscow. It was a policy that represented a virtual negation of the idea of non-alignment in the Cold War.

In the context of post-1945 American alliance policy, a Cold War neutral, particularly one located in a theater of active Russian-American confrontation, came to be looked at as intellectually unacceptable if not literally inconceivable. America, it is true, was forced over time to deal with a number of major neutral states, and at times to some advantage (Burma, Indonesia, Egypt, Ghana, and Sweden come immediately to mind), but this in no way alleviated the discomfort felt in Washington in the face of many of their attitudes. Secretary Dulles was especially prone to this type of reasoning, but one that was not unique with him.

Destructive political fallout from a continuing uneasiness and indecisiveness with such neutrality would remain throughout the Cold War era. America's historic relationship with India is a particularly graphic example of misplaced priorities in Washington's longtime conception of this matter, one result being an extended marriage of convenience between democratic India and

Soviet Russia lasting many years. Some of the most difficult decisions of American foreign policy over time consisted of choosing between developing a positive relationship with a disaffected Third World and maintaining its pristine alliance rationale intact. This would be keenly reflected in the country's approach toward the Philippines, Thailand, and South Korea in the face of deteriorating popular support for the military dictatorships in those countries.

Finally, America's alliance rationale represented a triumph of means over ends. It was not long before a kind of mystique developed around America's alliances, causing the country to place more emphasis on the alliances themselves than on the purposes that these arrangements were supposed to serve. With the commencement of the institutionalization process in the early 1950s, so large did alliances loom in American thinking and action that the maintenance of the fragile web of coalition diplomacy itself became a major end of policy. This was exemplified most cogently in Washington's disconcerting tendency to seek to uphold alliance cohesion by means of constant consultation. Each region, it was felt, should speak with one voice. A multiplicity of voices would give the illusion of disunity to the Russians, who might then be tempted to play the role of devil's advocate. Major problems flowed from this situation.

For one thing, consultation in the interests of cohesion often inhibited the capacity of the allies to reconcile their different needs with an efficacious strategy for all. What is more, Washington's urge for cohesion tended to be based strictly on American terms. To America, all the priority political decisions facing the non-communist West were made in the first decade after 1945, culminating in the decision to contain communism by force of arms, if necessary. American policy toward its alliances after that time would amount to little more than attempts to implement these basic decisions, always with a weather eye out for intrabloc unity. Thus, the military questions arising from the original political consensus (however superficial) that formed the basis of its postwar security remained in American eyes the primary task of its alliances, despite the fact the initial consensus had begun to erode almost from the beginning. In the process, it would be an impertinence for our allies to discuss the political goals for which the Cold War was presumably being waged.[11]

As long as the various allies viewed Russian "aggression" as a probable threat and as long as they required an American military presence to defend themselves, most of America's alliance partners were willing to support American leadership in order to receive our aid. As the Russian threat over time came to be seen as less probable by others, alliance members began to demonstrate more independence and less willingness to rely solely on America. Indeed, beginning with the French challenge in the 1960s, overt disagreements about, and even hostility toward, the original presumptions would persist.[12]

There is another price that America would pay for its insistence upon intra-alliance unity and support. Some of our smaller allies from time to time demanded higher payoffs to be enticed to stay within the alliance. In almost every instance, these demands were much too high in the light of the paucity of military capability they could contribute. In such cases, these small states usually created a drain on the alliance's capabilities rather than contributing to the coalition's overall strength. But as long as America continued to view the world from a Cold War perspective, the presence of small states in our regional alliances was seen as absolutely necessary.

In a few cases, America's allies even succeeded in "blackmailing" the bloc leader, extracting commitments for increased economic and military aid, which they then proceeded to use for purposes contrary to the American national purpose. Such was the case with Portugal, which for many years, as a member of NATO, was able to generate leverage in terms of its colonial policies in Africa. The classic illustration, of course, remains France's ability in the late 1940s and early 1950s to parlay American security concerns in Western Europe into support for its colonialist policies in Indochina.

Then, too, there is the question of compatible internal systems. Logically speaking, by artificially drawing a dividing line between freedom and communism, it was only natural, one supposes, that America would go one step further and assume that all the allied states shared the same basic policy priorities and interests, if not precisely the same values, in their respective lifestyles. In some instances, the bird came home to roost. In the case of Greece, American support for the "dictatorship of the colonels" in the late 1960s and early 1970s helped pave the way for a later strained relationship between these two states.

Most important, however, the greatest loss inherent in the emphasis on means was America's reluctance to address the heart of the matter—the problems posed by Soviet Russia. In a word, the country's oft-exhibited desire to hammer out a united front on every major substantive issue came to substitute for realistic negotiations with the Russians themselves. Indeed, the major tactical effort of American foreign policy throughout most of the post-1945 period would not be directed at the "Russian threat" at all but, rather, the creation and elaboration of a single anti-communist camp led by America as an integral part of a policy aimed at frustrating Moscow's alleged expansionist tendencies.

The American response to disengagement proposals during the 1954–1958 period is a case in point. Our initial response was to dismiss them, then under Allied pressure to agree to negotiate, and, finally, to obstruct them altogether by transforming NATO into an offensively armed alliance. The Eisenhower administration continued to push at this time for a rapid military buildup in NATO, all the while seeking to shore up the rest of its alliances in the face of increasing indications of change in the international milieu.[13] Yet even while pursuing its militant anti-communist policy throughout the world, Eisenhower and Dulles sought continuously to play down the more blatant aspects of American power, insisting, on the one hand, upon equality within its alliances while, on the other hand, opting for the principle of non-intervention in the affairs of sovereign states. The fact of the matter was, however, that America, while technically just one ally in a set of alliances, was in actuality a superstate aligned with many lesser states. Herein resided the chief difficulty, apart from the problem of what to do about Soviet Russia, that would plague the actual operation of America's alliances for many years. The successful conduct of an alliance on the basis of equality of its members presupposes that the identity of interests among the allies and their awareness of this identity are so complete that they will pursue common interests with common measures through spontaneous cooperation. In the degree that reality falls short of this assumption, the alliance operates less effectively.

All of this should not be surprising when one remembers that the American strategic orientation toward negotiation of issues with the Russians stressed a piecemeal approach. There was no necessary reason in logic why this fractioning of strategy should obscure long-term goals, but this in fact resulted. As the Cold War developed, American strategy increasingly came to concentrate upon the particular issue of the moment. The ultimate national purpose of the nation came to be blurred by successive overlays of response to the exigencies of recurrent crisis. The folly of this perception of America's primary role in the world lay in the fact that it inherently represented a view no larger or broader than a single conflict situation and thereby allowed a simplistic concept (and the hope that time would change things) to substitute for enlightened grand strategy.

RECAPITULATION

After World War II America became caught up in an interventionist policy—a strategy predicated by its leaders on a conviction that the affairs of the world were to be best understood in terms of a universal conflict of values involving the forces of international communism led by Soviet Russia and those of the free world. Pursuant to an evolving new operational notion of global responsibility, America consequently became active in virtually every sphere of international affairs. An integral part of this process was the creation of a vast complex of alliances and regional institutions, all the while solidifying American hegemony in areas regarded as its traditional spheres of influence. Beginning in 1947, the Rio de Janeiro Pact, the Truman Doctrine, the North Atlantic Treaty, the ANZUS Pact, the Southeast Asia Collective Defense Treaty, the Caracas and Taiwan Resolutions, the Baghdad Pact, and the Eisenhower Doctrine all marked distinct but related steps in a policy that appeared unable to articulate any purpose other than preventing a military expansion of the Russian sphere of influence—all at the expense of ignoring numerous, palpable opportunities to successfully manage the conflict at lower levels of intensity, if not settle it altogether.[14] One can only conclude that the rhetoric of response, that is to say, the quantification of means over ends, was allowed in the end to dictate the policy followed by America toward Soviet Russia.

In all of these activities, three common denominators came to be emphasized: America has global duties and responsibilities; America stands as the doorkeeper of freedom and morality on the world stage; and the future viability and peace of the world are dependent upon America's willingness and readiness to act abroad for the good of humankind. The grand strategy of a free society, however, should always take a view broader than a single conflict situation. In the final analysis, amelioration of that challenge to America resulted from a situational change brought about by the interplay of long-range and short-term historic forces—not, more generally, as a result of the application of America's containment rationale or, more specifically, its approach to alliances.

NOTES

1. Consider the zeal with which America collected some forty allies in the post-1945 era. In the United Nations Organization of the 1990s some one fifth of its members are still formal allies of America.

2. On this point, see Walter Lippmann's critique in *The Cold War: A Study in United States Foreign Policy* (New York: Macmillan, 1947).

3. For some general discussions of alliances and American foreign policy under Truman, Eisenhower, Kennedy, and Johnson, consult: Arnold Wolfers, *Alliance Policy in the Cold War* (Baltimore: Johns Hopkins University Press, 1959); Robert E. Osgood, *NATO: The Entangling Alliance* (Chicago: University of Chicago Press, 1962), and his *Alliances and American Foreign Policy* (Baltimore: Johns Hopkins University Press, 1968); Max Beloff, *The United States and the Unity of Europe* (Washington, D.C.: Brookings Institution, 1963); Francis A. Beer, *Integration and Disintegration in NATO* (Columbus: Ohio State University Press, 1969) and his *Alliances: Latent War Communities in the Contemporary World* (New York: Holt, Rinehart and Winston, 1970).

4. See Dean Acheson's congressional testimony, U.S. Senate, *North Atlantic Treaty*, Senate Committee Hearings, 1 (Washington, D.C.: Government Printing Office, 1949), pp. 20–27.

5. The Article 51 strategy at San Francisco was largely the work of two individuals—Nelson Rockefeller, Assistant Secretary of State for Latin America, and Senator Arthur H. Vandenburg, senior Republican member of the Senate Foreign Relations Committee. According to David Green, *The Containment of Latin America* (Chicago: Quadrangle Books, 1971), p. 234, Rockefeller wanted America to control its own sphere. Unless, he said, the U.S. "operated with a solid group in this hemisphere, it could not do what we wanted to do on the world front."

While Vandenburg wanted the Atlantic Charter freedoms universalized, Secretary of War Henry L. Stimson was virtually alone in opposing this orientation, criticizing those Americans "anxious to hang on to exaggerated views of the Monroe Doctrine and at the same time butt into every question that comes up in Central Europe." See Henry L. Stimson and McGeorge Bundy, *On Active Service in Peace and War* (New York: W. W. Norton, 1948), pp. 605–611.

6. See testimony before the Congress in which Truman administration witnesses sought to draw a clear distinction between the North Atlantic Treaty and traditional military alliances. John Foster Dulles stated, "I do not interpret this as a military alliance. If I thought it were a military alliance, I would oppose it unqualifiedly." Dean Acheson put it this way: "The idea of arrangements to prevent aggression is somewhat modern. In the old treaties it was if you became involved in

war, then the other signatory party would come to your help. . . . The conception of this treaty, and the conception of the Rio Treaty, and the conception of the Brussels Treaty is a newer one, and one which grows out of the principles and procedures of the U. N. Charter." Dulles' comments are taken from U.S. Senate Committee on Foreign Relations, *Hearings on NATO*, Part II,   81st Cong. 1st Sess, (Washington, D.C.: Government Printing Office, 1949), p. 231. Acheson's commentary may be found in ibid., Part I, pp. 14–15.

7. While America's distrust of the balance of power acquired an interesting set of guises historically, after 1945 these misgivings were manifested in a new rationalization as part of the country's rapid rise to superpower status.   A bipolar world was more stable, it was argued, and therefore more preferable than the "delicate" European balance of power arrangement used to be. A world organized into two great power systems was a better world than a world of several major players, "all roughly equal in strength," with, according to John Fisher, an "almost infinite opportunity for intrigue and combination, uneasiness about neighbors, shifting alliances and dangerous maneuver." See his views in Norman A. Graebner, ed., *Ideas and Diplomacy: Readings in the Intellectual Tradition of American Foreign Policy* (New York: Oxford University Press, 1964), p. 683. Kenneth Waltz would be a leading exponent of this thesis. See his "The Stability of a Bipolar World," *Daedalus* (Summer,1964): 881–909, and his *Theory of International Politics* (Reading, Mass.: Addison-Wesley Publishing Co., 1979).

John Lewis Gaddis has posited the notion that the absence of war between the two superpowers after 1945 led to an era which he characterized as the "long peace." The two primary reasons for this period of relative calm were the bipolar structure of the global system—a situation that accurately reflected the distribution of military power in the system as a whole—and more stable alliances because the bipolar system was a simple structure, easier to maintain than a multipolar one. Defections from the two blocs, consequently, did not cause major disruptions. See his *The Long Peace: Inquiries into the History of the Cold War* (New York: Oxford University Press, 1987).

There may well be, however, some empirical and conceptual difficulties in this "globalist" line of argument, not the least of which is the fact that there took place during these years many militarized interstate disputes and wars—all representing major sources of instability in the system. On this point, see Melvin M. Small and J. David Singer, *Resort to Arms: International and Civil Wars, 1816–1982* (Beverly Hills, Calif.: Sage, 1982); Charles S. Gochman and Zeev Maoz, "Militarized Interstate Disputes, 1816–1976: Procedures, Patterns, and Insights," *Journal of Conflict Resolution* 28 (December, 1984), pp. 585–616; and Manus Midlarsky, "Polarity and International Stability," *American Political Science Review* 87 (March, 1993), pp. 173–177.

A second difficulty with Gaddis' argument is the narrow scope of his definition of peace—one that excludes proxy wars, in which Soviet Russia and America were engaged in overt conflict through clients, as with Cuba and the Angolan civil war (1975–1988), or with the Contras and the Sandinista government in Nicaragua in the 1980s. It also excludes wars in which one superpower was a direct participant and the other was involved through direct military aid and/or covert support for its opponents, as in the Korean (1950–1953) and Afghanistan (1979–1989) conflicts.

A third conceptual problem is the equating of instability with war, and of non-war between the superpowers with global stability. Gaddis and others epitomize a literature on conflict that is skewed to the presence or absence of war as the sole indicator of (in)stability, failing to point out that many international conflicts do not involve overt violence and yet still pose grave challenges to system stability (for example, the three major crises involving Berlin—the Blockade [1948–1949], the Deadline [1957–1959], the Wall [1961]—and the Cuban Missile Crisis [1962]).

For a cogent criticism of the bipolar, "long peace" model, see Michael Brecher and Jonathan Wilkenfeld, *Crisis, Conflict, and Instability* (Oxford: Pergamon Press, 1989). See also Michael Brecher, Patrick James and Johnathan Wilkenfeld, "Polarity and Stability: New Concepts, Indicators and Evidence," *International Interactions* 16, No. 1 (1990), pp. 49–80; Michael Brecher, Jonathan Wilkenfeld, and Sheila Moser, *Crises in the Twentieth Century*, Vol. 1: *Handbook of International Crises* (Oxford: Pergamon Press, 1988).

8. The framework for the author's use of the term commitment is taken from an excellent analysis by Franklin B. Weinstein, "The Concept of a Commitment in International Relations," *Journal of Conflict Resolution* (March, 1969), pp. 39–56. For an additional useful perspective on the subject, see J. L. Brierly, *The Basis of Obligation in International Law* (London: Oxford University Press, 1958).

9. According to Brian Crozier, Britain and France warned Washington in 1955 that if a Vietminh attack on the southern zone came after a South Vietnamese refusal to implement the election provision of the Geneva Agreements, they would not feel bound to act under SEATO. This was not, needless to say, the American interpretation of SEATO's obligations. See his "The Diem Regime in Southern Vietnam," in *Far Eastern Survey* (1955), pp. 49–56. For an additional American view of the nature of SEATO's collective security commitments, see *Hearings on S. 2793* before the Senate Committee on Foreign Relations, 89th Cong., 2nd Sess. (Washington, D.C.: Government Printing Office, 1966), p. 56.

10. Take, for example, the notion of individual and collective self-defense, which has always been explicitly permitted under Article 51 of the UN Charter. A major problem in this vein, however, has been where to place within the scope of international law so-called anticipatory self-defense. An examination of the scholarly literature on this question reveals that most scholars fall into one of two schools of thought: "restrictionists" who argue that Article 51 prohibits anticipatory self-defense, and the "counterrestrictionists," who refuse to accept this argument. Unfortunately, in the years since 1945 there has been no authoritative decision of an international adjudicatory body on this matter. Meanwhile, state practice has been mixed, with a number of states taking the position that it may be lawful to use force in advance of an actual armed attack. For useful discussions on one of the more troubling issues in twentieth century politics and law, see D. Bowett, in Ian Brownlie, ed., "The Use of Force in Self-Defence in International Law," *British Yearbook of International Law* 37, (1991), pp. 166–183; Oscar Schachter, "The Lawful Resort to Unilateral Use of Force," *Yale Journal of International Law* 10, (1985), pp. 271–293; and William V. O'Brien, "International Law and the Outbreak of War in the Middle East, 1967," *ORBIS* 11 (1967), pp. 716–731.

More generally, see Lincoln Bloomfield, *International Military Forces, Peace-keeping in an Armed and Disarming* World (Boston: Little, Brown, 1964); Benjamin B. Ferencz, "Defining Aggression: Where It Stands and Where It's Going,"

American Journal of International Law 66 (1972), pp. 491–508; Richard Falk, "On Legal Tests of Aggressive War," ibid., pp. 560–571; and James N. Rosenau, ed., *International Aspects of Civil Strife* (Princeton, N.J.: Princeton University Press, 1964). See also "The International Regulation of Internal Violence in the Developing Countries," *Proceedings, American Society of International Law* (April, 1966).

11. This problem was reflected persistently in America's relationship with Britain during the early Cold War era, a situation that is ably characterized by Robin Edmonds, *Setting the Mould: The United States and Britain, 1945–1950* (New York: W. W. Norton & Co., 1986). See also Bruce M. Russett, *Community and Contention: Britain and America in the Twentieth Century* (Cambridge: MIT Press, 1963), and Coral Bell, *The Debatable Alliance* (London: Oxford University Press, 1964).

12. On France's growing problems with and dissent from America's ongoing positions and interpretations, see Alastair Buchan, *Crisis Management: The New Diplomacy* (Boulogne-sur-Seine: Atlantic Institute, 1966). See also J. J. Servan-Schreiber, *The American Challenge* (New York: Avon Books, 1967) and Claude Julien, *America's Empire* (New York: Vintage Books, 1973).

13. The evidence for this view may be found in a variety of places. See in this regard George F. Kennan, *Russia, the Atom and the West* (London: Oxford University Press, 1958); M. Steven Fish, "After Stalin's Death: The Anglo-American Debate over a New Cold War," *Diplomatic History* (Fall, 1986), pp. 343–353; Robert Divine, *Eisenhower and the Cold War* (New York: Oxford University Press, 1981), and his *Blowing on the Wind: The Nuclear Test Ban Debate, 1954–1960* (New York: Norton, 1978); Philip Noel-Baker, *The Arms Race* (London: Atlantic, 1958); Charles E. Bohlen, *Witness to History, 1929–1969* (New York: Norton, 1973); and James W. Robinson, "Disengagement in Europe: An Evaluation of U.S. Policy," *Columbia Essays in International Affairs*, Andrew W. Cordier, ed. (New York: Columbia University Press, 1966), pp. 31–58.

14. This thesis is more fully developed in the author's forthcoming study of the origins of the Cold War entitled, *The Cold War in Retrospect: The Formative Years,* to be published by Greenwood Press in 1998.

CHAPTER 6

Reflections

Man is born to live, not to prepare for life.

—Boris Pasternak

The writer's interest in the preceding pages has been both to characterize and to put into perspective the historic tradition of American foreign policy. Our purpose in undertaking this review has been neither to denigrate America's transcendent merits nor to deny its great achievements but to describe the peculiarities that have flawed many of its accomplishments. The other side of the attributes whose defects we have discussed in these pages reveal, after all, America's great virtues: a remarkable self-confidence; a great capacity for creative action; an ability to organize, to solve problems, and to get things done by sustained energy and determination; a method that entails a considerable ability to adapt; a continuing desire to see certain admirable forms of international relations prevail; and most important, a long-standing commitment, despite its frequent contradictory behavior, to a national purpose of equality in freedom.

Yet there remains a litany of contradictions and paradoxes in America's dealings with the rest of the world. The differences here between Americans and others have been not so much the differences that normally separate human beings but those between nations caught in different historical situations. It does little good to talk of these differences in terms of hypocrisy, imposture, or conspiracy. A hypocrite is a person who feigns beliefs or feelings that one does not possess; an impostor is someone who pretends to be something other than what one is. A conspirator is one who acts in some Machiavellian, treacherous, evil fashion. Things in America are not so easy; they go much deeper. A fundamental problem with American foreign policy stems from the fact that so many of its most important traditions and decision-making styles point simultaneously in opposite directions. No amount of engaging in conspiracy theories can detract from the hard truths of this reality.

AMERICA'S VALUES AND STYLE: A PERSISTING INCOMPATIBILITY

That there have been disconcerting and even destructive contradictions among many of the country's values and its operative national style is apparent. To an even greater degree than its propensity for misperception, America's habits of action have repeatedly frustrated the realization of its most wholesome values. Here, the faults that have plagued the nation in its dealings with others are more often than not ones of emphasis rather than of concept or intent.

There is, for example, the fact of America's self-righteousness. Out of the original optimism, egalitarianism, and the blessings of a new land for a select few there emerged a national sense of zealousness and uprightness that persists down to the present day. America was a new nation in a new world beyond the seas. Immigrants landing on its shores found surcease from the debilitating conflicts, the vices, poverty, and frustrations of the old world. Europe was the charnel house from which they fled. A sense of escape and freedom from evil was from the outset reinforced by a religious ingredient shared by believers and unbelievers alike.

This persistent national self-righteousness was to live on through American history as a permanent characteristic of our dealings with other nations and to express itself in a plenitude of expansive and vainglorious political dreams: America as the citadel of liberty, Manifest Destiny, a world made safe for democracy, the American century, a global great society. While even the skeptic must acknowledge that the best features of American society would not be a bad foundation for a better world, what has been so destructive of the nation's sense of direction for the last half of the twentieth century has been the spirit in which America's finest principles have been conveyed. It was up to others to relate to us; not up to us to relate to others. What other nations have required is an appreciation of what we represent and what we have accomplished, not mutual understanding.[1]

An even more pronounced dichotomy has been an enduring clash between the two dominant motifs in the Puritan ideology. There is, on the one hand, the most precious ideals of that heritage such as the beliefs in the dignity of the individual human being, one's right to dissent, and one's freedom to determine one's own destiny unfettered by undue interference from the state. It was this component of Puritanism as a kind of theological formulation of individualism and equality that ultimately in a secular form became the basis of the liberal democratic experiment in this country. On the other hand, there is the restrictive mood and suffocating strictures of many of the dynamics of that heritage. Even today there exists pronounced tension between the more rational elements of the heritage and some of the more retrograde aspects such as its fundamentalism, its tendency to mind other people's business, and its stifling moralism.

The consequences of the Puritan style, in contrast to its more admirable substance, have not infrequently been perverse in American history. What J. William Fulbright once called America's "intolerant Puritanism" has led the American people to stride through the world as if driven to subdue the sin of man.[2] These driving forces have, in turn, caused America to transform virtually every war it has ever entered into a crusade, to dehumanize its opponents to justify the terrible weapons of its technology, to see principles where there are only interests, and conspiracy where there is only misfortune.

While the original fundamentalism has long since been modified and adapted, it is revealing to witness a revival of the fundamentalist genre in the America of the 1980s and 1990s. That revival is no random development; it reflects a very important aspect of the American historic experience, mirroring as it does a continuing frustration at being headed in the contemporary world. An explanation for one's troubles that stresses the loss of "simple things" in life and that urges the exorcising of devils in recompense is one that ought to give us pause. It is also an illusion. Some thirty years ago, one of the country's great theologians cautioned that "we can . . . take no satisfaction in the pervading religiosity of our nation. Much of it . . . aggravates, rather than mitigates the problems." Americans, said Reinhold Niebuhr, should stop believing in the "Santa Clause" of simple moralistic solutions or the unrealistic power of undue reliance on positive thinking. We use evil in every moment of our existence to hold evil in check. An understanding of that elemental truth is essential for the establishment of a more humane planet.[3]

The habit of formulating the nation's world role in terms of mission is a particularly sensitive illustration of the marked contrast between the national purpose of the country and its decision-making style. To be sure, the missionary impulse in American history owes much to the sense of uniqueness and the moralist proclivities imbedded in the national psyche. The strong popular preference for the expression of America's goals as moral absolutes, as national missions, remains very much in vogue.

Remembering their unique orientation to the world, Americans have expected that the tasks accepted by their leaders in international affairs would naturally be of a higher and more lofty moral nature than would ordinarily be expected of a nation. The recurrence of the notion of crusade in the basic formulation of American foreign policy is not an accidental one. Recourse to this symbol signifies a strong belief on the part of virtually every American elite group that abstract principles of right and wrong form an important part of public consciousness. This tendency may be seen in the fondness of Americans traveling abroad to lecture other peoples on America's unique values and contributions and to insist that the salvation of the world lies in a global imitation of the American way. Moral principles have been consistently invoked throughout the country's history when departures from the "right way" were thought to have occurred; such departures must necessarily smack of appeasement.

Moreover, the kind of crusade on which Americans have periodically embarked has usually had more negative than positive results. Its long and durable anti-communism after 1945 is a case in point. During such crusades, the danger is that the specific and limited diplomatic interests of the nation become obscured in a larger campaign to reform the world politically—for example, to guarantee the four freedoms that will presumably in turn usher in a more peaceful and stable global order. Aside from the fact that these crusades have almost invariably caused great difficulties for the nation, they tend to bear some family resemblance to imperialism, particularly for societies that do not want to be "saved." Yet even today, America's statesmen are still inclined to believe that the surest way to build public support for their purposes is to assert a moral principle. In doing so, they have often exceeded the boundaries of propriety. At bottom, it is hard for Americans to comprehend that once ideology is projected into another nation-state, it becomes propaganda and is not necessarily perceived by others as the truth. It is in this context that we measure America's attempts over the years to extend its value system abroad. Such behavior, while appearing high-minded to us, often seems high-handed to others. The view that America's own experience is a beacon for mankind must thus confront the dilemma that an active foreign policy may just as surely create hostility as friendship on the part of others. This point is a difficult one for many Americans, for they believe that the country's foreign policies must win a net friendship in the long run to the degree that we remain faithful to the country's own fundamental ideals—values that are felt to be synonymous with humanity's goals.

The problem with this sort of reasoning is two fold: First, whether the country's interventions elsewhere in fact promote America's national purpose among other peoples is a debatable point; second, whether these interventions do not create more problems than they solve is open to question. One of the nation's most distinguished historians once observed, in reference to America's interventionist behavior in the Caribbean area, that "it is extremely doubtful whether the United States strengthens democracy . . . by active participation in the affairs of other states."[4] Except in rare instances, interventionists would be hard-pressed to demonstrate that their efforts have actually enhanced the prospects for the achievement of equality in freedom elsewhere. Moreover, the actual occurrences of intervention have created added burdens for the nation's foreign policy-makers. As often as not, our frequently clumsy interventionist efforts in foreign lands have left residues of resentment against this country.[5]

Its effect in many cases has been to discredit political movements associated with a foreign power. In both America and in the foreign country concerned, these attempts have usually led to aroused hopes and expectations that are almost always subsequently unfulfilled, thus engendering an attitude of disillusionment and frustration in each country. And when the cost becomes known of what it takes to encourage the growth of equality in freedom in other societies, leading the nation typically to refrain from paying it, America is denounced for being hypocritical. We are not, it is charged, sincerely devoted to the cause of political freedom abroad.

But the attractions of the moralist interventionist conception of mission continue to appeal. In the words of a Senate subcommittee,

The idea of manifest destiny still survives. Officials make sweeping declarations of our world mission, and often verbally commit the Nation to policies and programs far beyond our capabilities. . . . To some extent every post-war administration has indulged our national taste for the grand and even the grandiose. . . . The 'can do' philosophy accords with American folklore. . . . In policymaking, also, the assumption tends to be made that 'we can find the right way.'[6]

But Americans continue to believe that the fact that others have not yet come up to their standard does not mean that they cannot do so. Foreign peoples are thought to be attempting to follow the same general path of our development, only with less success. They are still believed to be innately disposed to acknowledge American leadership and example in the pursuit of the "common" goals of mankind except where they are tempted by the seductive allures of "false gods."

In all of this, several hard truths stand out: Americans have tended to be poor students of history, bad listeners, and chronically prone to oversimplify or downgrade foreign cultures. And, yet, bemused with gadgetry and frequently obsessed with physical and material power, if there was any final, fallback American quality in which we could justly take pride, it was our "know-how." Even if one studied nothing about a foreign culture, spoke no foreign language, or knew little of the "quaint" customs of others, people were people, weren't they? And they all want more abundant food, healthier children, contested elections and secret ballots, more effective police forces, and better roads, don't they?

And yet it happened that in country after country what we could do in America was not necessarily exportable; that we were not all that good at telling them how to organize their community life, conduct their politics, or educate their young. The record is full of instances of foreign aid pumped into the hands of elites who went about their merry way resisting agrarian reform and avoiding taxes, of machinery rusting in disuse after the technical mission left, of "self-defense" weaponry turned on their own people. The picture of the American idealist confidently trooping into a remote Third World village armed with universally applicable know-how replete with intrauterine loops and homilies on democracy continues to appeal.

The Resort to Violence

An even more pointed and disturbing contradiction between America's commitment to equality in freedom and the habits of action that have been derived from our historic experience remains the alacrity with which it resorts to violence.

Violence has been, in the memorable words of black power activist H. Rap Brown, "as American as cherry pie." Violence has a long history in America. The Puritans did not hesitate to employ it to intimidate those in the community who had strayed from the "right way." Humiliation, torture, and even death were instruments of the Lord, put in the hands of His righteous followers—men who believed that they had a special destiny on this planet to show other people the proper examples of godly living. Later, violence was frequently used against Indians, blacks, and white Americans in a civil war that was the bloodiest conflict of the nineteenth century. America's industrial entrepreneurs, sometimes with the assistance of the government, were not loath to deal violently with organized labor. Vigilantism long flourished on the frontier. A variety of "red-neck" groups like the Ku Klux Klan—all typically racist, anti-Catholic, and anti-Semite—have existed for many years. And through it all, the forces of law and order have on occasion dealt with protesting groups with severe measures.

What is remarkable about American history in this context is not so much the quality or even prevalence of its violence but the relative absence of permanent conflicts among ends that one finds and the patent unwillingness to tolerate such prolonged conflicts for very long. Because Americans have come to expect, even demand, harmony as the norm, the history of this country has borne frequent testimony to a propensity toward a national repression of issues on which there is no agreement but also no disagreement sufficient, it was felt, to justify violence.[7] But when the manifest division does not respond to these repressive measures, the commitment to restore the norm elicits the use of force. America's eagerness for harmony makes violence a necessary corollary. Consequently, violence in this country has historically tended to play the role of a kind of cleansing agent. Whenever genuine conflicts of purpose have cropped up from time to time, or when segments of the population have felt endangered, the urge to violence has manifested itself both on the part of the repressive majority and on the part of minorities that have often believed they had no other recourse.[8]

One of the unyielding facts of life in America is that there has often been little middle ground between the dominant thrust for harmony and consensus and the related violence in dissent. On the side of the "moral majority," the witch hunts and the monster chases are the signatures of a frustration that manifests itself in a kind of blind lashing out at wrongdoing rather than a compelling of the recalcitrants into new arrangements, as so often happens in other societies characterized by conflicts of purpose.[9] In many other

Western nations, for example, opposition to the dominant values of society has a way of being funneled through various institutions and competing belief systems.[10] But when there has occurred in America a "tyranny of the majority," when the only channels of dissent are circumscribed, the society has tended to be marked by a desperate, frenetic violence that epitomizes not only dissatisfaction but also the feeling of utter despair and the impatience of the "lonely crowd." An illustration of the continued urge among Americans for this sort of violence is their disconcerting habit of "knocking off" their presidents.

America's external experience has echoed this internal one: Conflicts of purpose between America and other nations have frequently ended with the stark imposition of force. The nation's wars with the Barbary Pirates, Britain, Mexico, Spain, Germany, Italy, Japan, North Korea, China, Vietnam, Grenada, and Iraq reflect in some fashion this trait. In employing violence in these instances, Americans have sought the elimination of conflict through the destruction of the "enemy." The propensity for violence has been the "axiomatic response" of a people whose amazing record of domestic consensus meant that endemic human conflict was long resented as an impertinence or imposition.[11]

Yet, ironically, America abhors the very violence that is its instinctive response. Grateful for its marvelous ability to assimilate diverse experiences and peoples, delighted in the fruits of its unique harmonious cultural arrangements, unyielding in its rejection of power politics, Americans truly believe that violence is wicked—an abomination in God's eyes. Insofar as there is a deep conviction in America that needlessly destructive conflicts of ends are not indispensable aspects of life, the only way therefore of reconciling America's cultural ideal to that reality is to make sacrosanct the resort to violence. In other words, the ultimate justification for violence in American history, in terms of the collective self-image of its people, has been the mitigating balm of its high principles. In the last analysis, violence is legitimized by one principle—one "golden rule"—which tends to incorporate and transcend all of America's values: the great belief in the possibility, the desirability, and the inevitability of a final elimination of conflicts of purpose from the affairs of mankind.

Only in this way may one begin to comprehend the enormity of this paradox. America's ideal of consensus, played out in the context of its habitual use of force, has compelled the nation into a kind of vicious circle with little respite for its people. To a considerable degree our foreign policy has come to rely on force, or the threat of force, to preserve and to promote the nation's purpose. But the moral dilemma remains: The use of violence for political ends is an "index of the failure of political authority."[12] This fact would be demonstrated again and again in the post-1945 conduct of America's foreign relations. The brutality of force, even when employed for lofty principles, has too often meant a corruption of the nation's goals and a negation of its purpose of equality in freedom.

The Necessity for Choice

America's limited ability to communicate articulately its greatest ideals in foreign affairs, and to act wisely on their behalf, stems in great measure from a lack of fundamental discontent among its people toward the international status quo that has prevailed throughout much of the twentieth century. America's acceptance of the "good life" in an international environment fraught with difficulty is obvious, for the comforts of the era of American hegemony in the world have been undeniably pleasurable for Americans. But, ironically, its contentment would breed a sea of troubles in the years after World War II, for the nation's effort to perpetuate the satisfying aspects of the present during the last half of the twentieth century led it into political overextension and to the adoption of destructive policies of reaction to the challenges to the status quo, from whatever quarter.

Moreover, it is those ideologies committed to the ushering in of a transmuted future (even if conceptualized as the continuation of the present) that have legitimized the most ruinous of conduct in the here and now. In this way, Americanism must be seen for what it has become: a supremely confident, self-possessed ideology of means that, in the last half of the twentieth century, turned many lands into vales of tears.

The twentieth century has seen an uneasy and anxious America saddled with the burdens of world involvement and preeminence. In the process of interacting with others during these years, it would become increasingly evident that many of the nation's most cherished traditions were found to be disembodied. Insofar as our norms have been grounded in political and social realities, it has only been in those of our own choosing, and many times those that have been stressed have not even been internally consistent.

He who does not profit from history's lessons is destined to repeat its mistakes; equally, he who visualizes history as simply recapitulation is doomed to failure. Nations, no less than individual human beings, need to both avoid neglecting history and overreacting to it. To most of us, genuine mutual understanding is denied to the very end of our lives. Much of human life on earth is a litany of missed opportunities, misperception of one another's intentions, and failure to understand what motivates others—an unending array of misconceptions and misunderstandings. And the more the decision-making process is set in the concrete of intransigent doctrines and stereotypes, the less likely we are to see genuine progress to higher levels of understanding.

NOTES

1. The purposes of the United Nations Charter in this sense have been American purposes writ large.

2. See J. William Fulbright, *The Arrogance of Power* (New York: Random House, 1966).

3. Cited in June Bingham, *Courage to Change* (New York: Charles Scribner's Sons, 1961), p. 361.

4. Dexter E. Perkins, *The United States and Latin America* (Baton Rouge: Louisiana State University Press, 1961), p. 19.

5. This has been especially true with regard to our many interventions in Latin America.

6. U.S. Senate, *Memorandum of the Subcommittee on National Security and International Operations*, Committee on Government Operations, 89th Cong., 1st sess. (Washington, D.C.: Government Printing Office, 1965), pp. 2–3. This, despite the fact that America tolerated slavery longer than Britain and France and that in these countries one does not find committees on un-English or un-French activities.

7. The questions concerning the use of drugs and the rights of women in the marketplace in the last three decades of the twentieth century certainly would seem to qualify as bona fide illustrations of this point.

8. See Stanley Hoffmann, *Gulliver's Troubles or the Setting of American Foreign Policy* (New York: McGraw-Hill, 1968), pp. 181–182.

9. Richard Hofstadter, in *The Paranoid Style in American Politics and Other Essays* (New York: Alfred A. Knopf, 1965), has brilliantly analyzed this psychological characteristic of the American people as demonstrated in their historical relationships.

10. This point is addressed by Gabriel A. Almond and Sidney Verba, *The Civic Culture. Political Attitudes and Democracy in Five Nations* (Princeton, N.J.: Princeton University Press, 1963).

11. Ernest R. May, "The Nature of Foreign Policy: The Calculated vs. the Axiomatic," *Daedalus* (Fall, 1962), pp. 653–667.

12. Hannah Arendt, *On Violence* (New York: Harcourt, Brace & World, 1970), p. 41.

Selected Bibliography

Listed here are only the writings that have been of particular value to the writer in the making of this book. This bibliography is by no means a complete accounting of all the works and other sources that I have consulted but, rather, reflects the substance and range of material taken into consideration in the formulation of my ideas and conclusions.

Adler, Selig. *The Uncertain Giant: 1921–1941, American Foreign Policy between the Wars.* New York: Macmillan, 1965.

Allison, Graham. *Essence of Decision: Explaining the Cuban Missile Crisis.* Boston: Little, Brown, 1971.

Almond, Gabriel. *The American People and Foreign Policy.* New York: Praeger, 1960.

Almond, Gabriel A., and Sidney Verba. *The Civic Culture. Political Attitudes and Democracy in Five Nations.* Princeton, N.J.: Princeton University Press, 1963.

Ambrose, Stephen E. *Rise to Globalism: American Foreign Policy since 1938.* 8th rev. ed. Baltimore: Penguin Books, 1997.

Appleton, Sheldon. *United States Foreign Policy: An Introduction with Cases.* Boston: Little, Brown, 1968.

Arendt, Hannah. *On Violence.* New York: Harcourt, Brace & World, 1970.

Bailey, Thomas A. *A Diplomatic History of the American People*, 8th ed. New York: Appleton-Century-Crofts, 1969.

Ball, George. "The Dangers of Nostalgia," *Department of State Bulletin,* April 12, 1965: 532–535.

Baritz, Loren. *City on the Hill: A History of Ideas and Myths in America.* New York: John Wiley & Sons, 1964.

Barnet, Richard J. *Roots of War: The Men and Institutions behind U.S. Foreign Policy.* New York: Atheneum, 1972.

Barnet, Richard J., and Ronald Mueller. *Global Reach: The Power of the Multi-national Corporation.* New York: Simon & Schuster, 1974.

Bartlett, Ruhl J. *The Record of American Diplomacy,* 4th ed. New York: Alfred A. Knopf, 1964.

Barzini, Luigi Giorgio. *Americans Are Alone in the World.* Freeport, N.Y.: Library Press, 1972.

Beard, Charles. *Giddy Minds and Foreign Quarrels.* New York: Macmillan, 1939.

Bemis, Samuel Flagg. *A Diplomatic History of the United States,* 5th ed. New York: Holt, Rinehart and Winston, Inc., 1965.

——. *The Diplomacy of the American Revolution.* Bloomington: Indiana University Press, 1957.

——. *The Latin American Policy of the United States.* New York: Harcourt, Brace & World, 1943.

Billington, Ray Allen. *Westward Expansion.* New York: Macmillan, 1949.

Bingham, June. *Courage to Change.* New York: Charles Scribner's Sons, 1961.

Blum, John M. *The Promise of America: An Historical Inquiry.* Boston: Houghton-Mifflin, 1966.

Bohlen, Charles E. *Witness to History, 1929–1969.* New York: Norton, 1973.

Boorstin, Daniel J. *America and the Image of Europe.* New York: Meridian Books, 1960.

——. *The Americans: The National Experience.* New York: Random House, 1965.

——. *The Genius of American Politics.* Chicago: University of Chicago Press, 1953.

Brauer, J. C. *Reflections on the Nature of English Puritanism.* Boston: Beacon Press, 1954.

Brecher, Michael, and Jonathan Wilkenfeld. *Crisis, Conflict, and Instability.* Oxford: Pergamon Press, 1989.

Brecher, Michael, Patrick James, and Jonathan Wilkenfeld. "Polarity and Stability: New Concepts, Indicators, and Evidence," *International Interactions* 16, No. 1 (1990): 49–80.

Brecher, Michael, Jonathan Wilkenfeld, and Sheila Moser. *Crises in the Twentieth Century,* Vol. 1, *Handbook of International Crises.* Oxford: Pergamon Press, 1988.

Brogan, Denis W. *American Aspects.* New York: Harper & Row, 1964.

——. *The American Character,* rev. ed. New York: W. W. Norton, 1944.

——. "The Illusion of American Omnipotence," *Harpers* 205 (December, 1952): 21–28.

Burns, Edward. *The American Idea of Mission. Concepts of National Purpose.* Westport, Conn.: Greenwood Press, 1957.

Burt, Alfred Leroy. *The United States, Great Britain and British North America from the Revolution to the Establishment of Peace after the War of 1812.* New York: Russell and Russell, 1961.

Campbell, John Franklin. *The Foreign Affairs Fudge Factory.* New York: Bobbs-Merrill, 1972.

Clemens, Diane Shaver. *Yalta.* New York: Oxford University Press, 1970.

Cline, Howard F. *The United States and Mexico,* rev. ed. Cambridge, Mass.: Harvard University Press, 1963.

Cohen, Bernard C. *The Public's Impact on Foreign Policy.* Boston: Little, Brown, 1973.

Cohen, Warren I. *America's Response to China: An Interpretative History of Sino-American Relations.* New York: Wiley, 1971.

Coleman, Lee. "What Is American? A Study of Alleged American Traits," *Social Forces* 19 (May, 1941): 492–499.

Commager, Henry Steele. *America in Perspective: The United States through Foreign Eyes.* New York: Mentor Books, 1948.

——. *The American Mind: An Interpretation of American Thought and Character Since the 1880s.* New Haven, Conn.: Yale University Press, 1950.

Crabb, Cecil V. *American Diplomacy and the Pragmatic Tradition.* Baton Rouge: Louisiana State University Press, 1989.

——. *American Foreign Policy in the Nuclear Age.* New York: Harper & Row, 1960.

——. *Doctrines of American Foreign Policy: Their Meaning, Role, and Future.* Baton Rouge: Louisiana State University Press, 1982.

——. *Policy-Makers and Critics: Conflicting Theories of American Foreign Policy.* New York: Praeger, 1976.

Crèvecoeur, Hector St. John. *Letters from an American Farmer.* Everyman's Library edition. New York: E. P. Dutton, 1912.

Davis, Lynn Etheridge. *The Cold War Begins: Soviet-American Conflict over Eastern Europe.* Princeton, N.J.: Princeton University Press, 1974.

Deutsch, Karl W., and Richard L. Merritt. "Effects of Events on National and International Images," in Herbert Kelman, ed., *International Behavior: A Social-Psychological Analysis.* New York: Holt, Rinehart and Winston, 1965.

Divine, Robert A. *Blowing on the Wind: The Nuclear Test Ban Debate, 1954–1960.* New York: Norton, 1978.

——. *Eisenhower and the Cold War.* New York: Oxford University Press, 1981.

——. *The Illusion of Neutrality.* Chicago: University of Chicago Press, 1962.

Dulles, Foster Rhea. *China and America: The Story of Their Relations since 1784.* Princeton, N.J.: Princeton University Press, 1946.

Dulles, John Foster. *War or Peace.* New York: Macmillan, 1950.

Edelman, Murray. *The Symbolic Uses of Politics.* Urbana: University of Illinois Press, 1967.

Ekirch, Arthur A., Jr. *Ideas, Ideals and American Diplomacy.* New York: Appleton-Century-Crofts, 1966.

Ellis, Louis E. *Frank B. Kellogg and American Foreign Relations, 1925–1929.* New Brunswick, N.J.: Rutgers University Press, 1961.

Erikson, Robert, and Norman Luttbeg. *American Public Opinion.* New York: Wiley, 1973.

Fairbank, John K. *The United States and China,* rev. ed. New York: Viking Press, 1948.

Falk, Richard. "Janus Tormented," in James Rosenau, ed., *International Aspects of Civil Strife.* Princeton, N.J.: Princeton University Press, 1971: 185–248.

Falk, Richard, ed. *The Vietnam War and International Law.* Princeton, N.J.: Princeton University Press, 1969.

Farber, Maurice L. "The Problem of National Character: A Methodological Analysis," *Journal of Psychology* 30 (1950): 307–316.

Ferrell, Robert H. *American Diplomacy in the Great Depression: Hoover-Stimson Foreign Policy, 1929–1933.* New Haven, Conn.: Yale University Press, 1957.

Finlay, Moses I. *The Use and Abuse of History.* New York: Viking Press, 1975.

Fish, M. Steven. "After Stalin's Death: The Anglo-American Debate over a New Cold War," Diplomatic History, Fall, 1986: 343–353.

Fisher, Roger. *International Conflict for Beginners,* rev. ed. New York: Peter Smith Publishers, 1985.

Fukyama, Francis. "The End of History?" *National Interest* (Summer, 1989): 21–40.

Fulbright, J. William. *Old Myths and New Realities.* New York: Random House, 1964.

——. *The Arrogance of Power.* New York: Random House, 1966.

Fyfe, Henry Hamilton. *The Illusion of National Character.* London: Watts and Co., 1940.

Gabriel, Ralph Henry. *The Course of American Democratic Thought since 1815.* New York: Ronald Press Co., 1940.

Gaddis, John Lewis. *The Long Peace: Inquiries into the History of the Cold War.* New York: Oxford University Press, 1987.

Gardner, Lloyd C., Walter F. LeFeber, and Thomas J. McCormick. *The Creation of the American Empire: United States Diplomatic History.* Chicago: Rand McNally, 1973.

Garson, Robert. "The Atlantic Alliance, Eastern Europe, and the Origins of the Cold War," *Bicentennial Essays in Anglo-American History.* New York: Macmillan, 1976: 296–320.

Gazley, John G. *American Opinion of German Unification, 1848–1871.* New York: Columbia University Press, 1926.

Gilbert, Felix. *To the Farewell Address: Ideas of Early American Foreign Policy.* Princeton, N.J.: Princeton University Press, 1961.

Goldman, Eric F. *Rendezvous with Destiny.* New York: Alfred A. Knopf, 1953.

Goldwin, Robert A., ed. *Left, Right and Center: Essays on Liberalism and Conservatism in the United States.* Chicago: Rand McNally, 1967.

Goodman, Allan. *The Lost Peace: America's Search for a Negotiated Settlement of the Vietnam War.* Palo Alto, Calif.: Hoover Institute, 1978.

Goodman, Warren H. "The Origins of the War of 1812: A Survey of Changing Interpretations," *Mississippi Valley Historical Review* 28 (September, 1941): 171–186.

Gorer, Geoffrey. *The American People: A Study in National Character,* rev. ed. New York: W. W. Norton, 1964.

Gouldner, Alvin. "Prologue to a Theory of Revolutionary Intellectuals," *TELOS,* No. 26 (Winter, 1975–1976): 3–36.

Graber, Doris A. *Crisis Diplomacy: A History of U.S. Intervention Policies and Practices.* Washington, D.C.: Public Affairs Press, 1959.

Graebner, Norman A. *Empire on the Pacific: A Study in American Continental Expansion.* New York: Ronald Press, 1955.

——. "Isolationism," *International Encyclopedia of the Social Sciences* 8. New York: Crowell, Collier and Macmillan, 1968: 218–219.

——, ed. *Ideas and Diplomacy: Readings in the Intellectual Tradition of American*

Foreign Policy. New York: Oxford University Press, 1964.

Green, David. *The Containment of Latin America.* Chicago: Quadrangle Books, 1971.

Gulick, Edward Vose. *Europe's Classical Balance of Power.* Ithaca, N.Y.: Cornell University Press, 1955.

Hackett, Charles W. *The Mexican Revolution and the United States, 1910–1926.* Boston: World Peace Foundation, 1926.

Hartmann, Frederick H. *The New Age of American Foreign Policy.* New York: Macmillan, 1970.

Hartz, Louis. *The Liberal Tradition in America: An Interpretation of American Political Thought since the Revolution.* New York: Harcourt, Brace and World, 1955.

——, ed. *The Founding of New Societies.* New York: Harcourt, Brace, 1964.

Healy, David. *United States Expansionism: The Imperialist Urge in the 1890's.* Madison: University of Wisconsin Press, 1970.

Herring, George. "The War in Vietnam," in Robert Divine, ed., *Exploring the Johnson Years.* Austin: University of Texas Press, 1981.

Herz, Martin. *Beginnings of the Cold War.* New York: McGraw-Hill, 1966.

Herzon, Frederick D., "Intensity of Opinion and the Organization of Political Attitudes," *Western Political Quarterly* 28, No. 1 (March, 1975): 72–84.

Hobson, J. A. *Imperialism: A Study,* 3rd ed. London: George Allen and Unwin, 1938.

Hoffmann, Stanley. *Gulliver's Troubles or the Setting of American Foreign Policy.* New York: McGraw-Hill, 1968.

Hofstadter, Richard. *The Paranoid Style in American Politics and Other Essays.* New York: Alfred A. Knopf, 1965.

Holsti, Ole R. "The Belief System and National Images: A Case Study," *Journal of Conflict Resolution* 6, No. 3 (September, 1962): 245–271.

Houghton, Neil. *Struggle Against History: U.S. Foreign Policy in an Age of Revolution.* New York: Simon & Schuster, 1968.

Hoy, Edwin C. *Law and Force in American Foreign Policy.* Lanham: University Press of America, 1985.

Hughes, Barry B. *The Domestic Context of American Foreign Policy.* San Francisco: Freeman, 1978.

Hunt, Michael H. *Ideology and U. S. Foreign Policy.* New Haven, Conn.: Yale University Press, 1987.

Huthmacher, J. Joseph. *A Nation of Newcomers: Ethnic Minority Groups in American History.* New York: Dell, 1967.

Inkeles, Alex, and Daniel J. Levinson. "National Character: The Study of Modal Personality and Sociocultural Systems," *Handbook of Social Psychology* 11. Reading, Mass.: Addison-Wesley, 1954.

Jervis, Robert. *Perception and Misperception in International Politics.* Princeton N.J.: Princeton University Press, 1976.

Julien, Claude. *America's Empire.* New York: Random House, 1973.

Kaplan, Lawrence S. *American Foreign Policy in the Age of Jefferson.* Kent, Ohio: Kent State University Press, 1987.

Kearns, Doris. *Lyndon Johnson and the American Dream.* New York: Harper, 1976.

Keniston, Kenneth. *The Uncommitted.* New York: Harcourt, Brace, 1965.

Kennan, George F. *American Diplomacy, 1900–1950.* New York: Mentor Books, 1952.

——. *Realities of American Foreign Policy.* Princeton, N J.: Princeton University Press, 1954.

——. *Russia, the Atom and the West.* London: Oxford University Press, 1958.

Kissinger, Henry. *A World Restored: Metternich, Castlereagh, and the Problem of Peace.* Boston: Houghton-Mifflin Co., 1957.

——. *Diplomacy.* New York: Simon & Schuster, 1994.

Koch, Adrienne. *Power, Morals and the Founding Fathers: Essays on the Interpretation of the American Enlightenment.* Ithaca, N.Y.: Great Seal Books, 1961.

Kohn, Hans. *American Nationalism: An Interpretative Essay.* New York: Macmillan, 1957.

Kolko, Gabriel. *The Roots of American Foreign Policy.* Boston: Beacon Press, 1969.

Kraslow, David, and Stuart Loory. *The Secret Search for Peace in Vietnam.* New York: Random House, 1968.

LaFeber, Walter. *America, Russia, and the Cold War,* 5th ed. New York: Alfred A. Knopf, 1985.

——. *The New Empire: An Interpretation of American Expansion, 1860–1898.* Ithaca, N.Y.: Cornell University Press, 1963.

Langer, William L., and S. Everett Gleason. *The Challenge to Isolation.* New York: Harper & Row, 1952.

——. *The Undeclared War.* New York: Harper & Row, 1953.

Larrabee, Stephen A. *Hellas Observed: The American Experience of Greece, 1775–1865.* New York: New York University Press, 1957.

Larson, David L. *The Puritan Ethic in U.S. Foreign Policy.* New York: Van Nostrand, 1966.

Leopold, Richard W. *The Growth of American Foreign Policy.* New York: Alfred A. Knopf, 1962.

Lengyel, Emil. *Americans from Hungary.* Philadelphia: Lippincott, 1948.

Lerche, Charles O., Jr. *Foreign Policy of the American People,* 3rd ed. Englewood Cliffs, N.J.: Prentice-Hall, 1967.

Lerner, Max. *America as a Civilization.* New York: Simon & Schuster, 1957.

——. *Ideas Are Weapons: The History and Uses of Ideas.* New York: Viking, 1939.

Lerski, Jerzy Jan. *A Polish Chapter in Jacksonian America: The United States and the Polish Exiles of 1831.* Madison: University of Wisconsin Press, 1958.

Lichtheim, George. *The Concept of Ideology and Other Essays.* New York: Random House, 1967.

Lippmann, Walter. *The Cold War: A Study in United States Foreign Policy.* New York: Macmillan, 1947.

——. *The Public Philosophy.* Boston: Little, Brown, 1955.

——. "The Rivalry of Nations," *Atlantic Monthly* 181 (February, 1948): 13–19.

Lipset, Seymour Martin. *The First New Nation: The United States in Historical and Comparative Perspective.* New York: Basic Books, 1963.

Magdoff, Harry. *The Age of Imperialism: The Economics of United States Foreign*

Policy. New York: Monthly Review Press, 1969.

Mannheim, Karl. *Ideology and Utopia.* New York: Harcourt, Brace & World, 1955.

May, Ernest R. *Imperial Democracy: The Emergence of America as a Great Power.* New York: Harcourt, Brace, Jovanovich, 1961.

——. *"Lessons" of the Past: The Use and Misuse of History in American Foreign Policy.* London: Oxford University Press, 1973.

——. "The Nature of Foreign Policy: The Calculated vs. the Axiomatic," *Daedalus* (Fall, 1962): 653–667.

Mead, Margaret. *And Keep Your Powder Dry: An Anthropologist Looks at America.* New York: William Morrow, 1942.

Mecham, J. Lloyd. *The United States and Inter-American Security, 1889–1960.* Austin: University of Texas Press, 1961.

Mencken, H. L. *Notes on Democracy.* New York: John Putnam & Sons, 1926.

Merk, Frederick. *Manifest Destiny and Mission in American History: A Reinterpretation.* New York: Alfred A. Knopf, 1963.

——. *The Monroe Doctrine and American Expansionism, 1843–1849.* New York: Alfred A. Knopf, 1966.

Midlarsky, Manus. "Polarity and International Stability," *American Political Science Review* 87 (March, 1993): 173–177.

Miller, Perry. "From the Covenant to the Revival," in J. W. Smith and A. L. Jamison, eds., *The Shaping of American Religion.* Boston: Beacon Press, 1958: 24–38.

Morgan, H. Wayne. *America's Road to Empire: The War with Spain and Overseas Expansion.* New York: Wiley, 1965.

Morgenthau, Hans J. "The Mainsprings of American Foreign Policy: The National Interest vs. Moral Abstractions," *American Political Science Review* (December, 1950): 833–854.

Morley, Felix. *The Foreign Policy of the United States.* New York: Alfred A. Knopf, 1951.

Morris, Bernard S. *International Communism and American Foreign Policy.* New York: Atherton Press, 1966.

Nie, Norman. "Mass Belief Systems Revisited: Political Change and Attitude Structure," *Journal of Politics* 36, No. 3 (August, 1974): 540–591.

Niebuhr, Reinhold, and Alan Heimert. *A Nation So Conceived.* New York: Charles Scribner's Sons, 1963.

Noel-Baker, Philip. *The Arms Race.* London: Atlantic, 1958.

Notter, Harley. *The Origins of the Foreign Policy of Woodrow Wilson.* Baltimore: Johns Hopkins University Press, 1937.

Osgood, Robert E. *Alliances and American Foreign Policy.* Baltimore: Johns Hopkins University Press, 1968.

——. *NATO: The Entangling Alliance.* Chicago: University of Chicago Press, 1962.

Page, Kirby. *National Defense.* New York: Macmillan, 1968.

Paine, Thomas. *Common Sense 1776.* Nelson F. Adkins, ed. Indianapolis, Ind.: Bobbs-Merrill, 1953.

Palmer, Robert. *Age of the Democratic Revolution, 1760–1800.* 2 vols. Princeton, N.J.: Princeton University Press, 1959.

Parkes, Henry Bamford. *The American Experience.* New York: Alfred A. Knopf,

1947.

Perkins, Bradford. *Prologue to War: England and the United States, 1805–1812.* Berkeley: University of California Press, 1961.

Perkins, Dexter. *Hands Off: A History of the Monroe Doctrine.* Boston: Little, Brown, 1941.

——. *The American Approach to Foreign Policy.* Cambridge: Harvard University Press, 1952.

——. *The United States and Latin America.* Baton Rouge: Louisiana State University Press, 1961.

Plamenatz, John. *Ideology.* New York: Praeger, 1970.

Pletcher, David M. *The Diplomacy of Annexation: Texas, Oregon, and the Mexican War.* Columbia: University of Missouri Press, 1973.

Potter, David. *People of Plenty.* Chicago: University of Chicago Press, 1954.

Pratt, Julius W. *A History of United States Foreign Policy,* 3rd ed. Englewood Cliffs, N.J.: Prentice-Hall, 1972.

——. *Expansionists of 1898.* Baltimore, Md.: Johns Hopkins University Press, 1936.

Quirk, Robert E. *An Affair of Honor: Woodrow Wilson and the Occupation of Veracruz.* Lexington: University of Kentucky Press, 1962.

Resis, Albert. "The Stalin-Churchill Secret 'Percentages' Agreement on the Balkans, Moscow, October, 1944," *American Historical Review* (April, 1978): 368–387.

Riesman, David. *The Lonely Crowd.* New Haven, Conn.: Yale University Press, 1950.

Robinson, Charles W. "Disengagement in Europe: An Evaluation of U.S. Policy," *Columbia Essays in International Affairs,* Andrew Cordier, ed. New York: Columbia University Press, 1966: 31–58.

Rosenau, James N., ed. *Domestic Sources of Foreign Policy.* New York: Free Press, 1967.

Rostow, Walt W. *The Process of Economic Growth.* New York: W. W. Norton & Co., 1952.

Russett, Bruce M., and Elizabeth C. Hanson. *Interest and Idelogy: The Foreign Policy Beliefs of American Businessmen.* San Francisco: W. H. Freeman and Co., 1975.

Saloutos, Theodore. *The Greeks in the United States.* Cambridge, Mass.: Harvard University Press, 1964.

Seabury, Paul. *Power, Freedom and Diplomacy: The Foreign Policy of the United States of America.* New York: Random House, 1963.

Small, Melvin M. *Was War Necessary? National Security and U.S. Entry into War.* Beverly Hills, Calif.: Sage Publications, 1980.

Small, Melvin M., and J. David Singer. *Resort to Arms: International and Civil Wars, 1816–1982.* Beverly Hills, Calif.: Sage Publications, 1982.

Smith, Daniel M., ed. *Major Problems in American Diplomatic History.* Boston: D. C. Heath & Co., 1964.

Smith, Don D. "Dark Areas of Ignorance Revisited," in Don D. Nimmo and Charles Bonjean, eds. *Political Attitudes and Public Opinion.* New York: McKay, 1972: 267–272.

Spiller, Robert E., and Eric Larabee, eds. *American Perspective: The National*

   Self-Image in the Twentieth Century. Cambridge: Harvard University
      Press, 1961.
Steel, Ronald. *Pax Americana.* New York: Viking Press, 1970.
Stephanson, Anders. *Manifest Destiny: American Expansion and the Empire of
      Right.* New York: Hill and Wang, 1995.
Stillman, Edmund, and William Pfaff. *Power and Impotence.* New York: Vintage
      Books, 1966.
Stinchcombe, William C. *The American Revolution and the French Alliance.*
      Syracuse, N.Y.: Syracuse University Press, 1969.
Tannenbaum, Frank. *The American Tradition in Foreign Policy.* Norman: Uni-
      versity of Oklahoma Press, 1955.
Taubman, William. *Stalin's American Policy: From Entente to Detente to Cold
      War.* New York: Norton, 1982.
Taubman, William, ed. *Globalism and Its Critics: The American Foreign Poli-
      cy Debate of the l960's.* Lexington, Mass.: D. C. Heath, 1973.
Taylor, A. J. P. *The Struggle for the Mastery of Europe, 1848–1918.* Oxford:
      Clarendon Press, 1960.
Thompson, Kenneth W. *Interpreters and Critics of the Cold War.* Washington,
      D.C.: University Press of America, 1978.
Tocqueville, Alexis de. *Democracy in America,* Phillips Bradley, ed. New York:
      Vintage Books, 1958.
Toynbee, Arnold. *America and the World Revolution.* London: Oxford University
      Press, 1962.
Turner, Frederick Jackson. "Contributions of the West to American Democracy,"
      The Frontier in American History. New York: Henry Holt and Co., 1920.
Walton, Richard. *Cold War and Counter-Revolution: The Foreign Policy of John
      F. Kennedy.* Baltimore: Penguin Books, 1972.
Waltz, Kenneth. "The Stability of a Bipolar World," *Daedulus* (Summer, 1964):
      881–909.
Webster, C. K. *The Foreign Policy of Castlereagh.* London: G. Bell and Sons,
      1947.
Weinberg, Albert K. "The Historical Meaning of the American Doctrine of Isola-
      tion," *American Political Science Review* (June, 1940): 101–148.
Weissberg, Robert G. *Public Opinion and Popular Government.* Englewood
      Cliffs, N.J.: Prentice-Hall, 1976.
Welch, William. *American Images of Soviet Foreign Policy.* New Haven, Conn.:
      Yale University Press, 1970.
Williams, Philip. *Crisis and Compromise.* Hamden, Conn.: Archon Books, 1964.
Williams, Raymond. *Culture and Society, 1780–1950.* Garden City, N.Y.: An-
      chor Books, 1960.
Williams, William Appleman. *America Confronts a Revolutionary World.* New
      York: William Morrow, 1976.
——, ed. *The Shaping of American Diplomacy.* Chicago: Rand McNally, 1956.
Wittke, Carl. *Refugees of Revolution: The German Forty-Eighters in America.*
      Philadelphia: University of Pennsylvania Press, 1952.
Wolfers, Arnold. *Alliance Policy in the Cold War.* Baltimore: Johns Hopkins Uni-
      versity Press, 1959.

Wolfers, Arnold, and Lawrence W. Martin, eds. *The Anglo-American Tradition in Foreign Affairs.* New Haven, Conn.: Yale University Press, 1956.

Index

About the Author

ROGER S. WHITCOMB is Professor of American International Relations and Foreign Policy Studies at Kutztown University of the Pennsylvania State System of Higher Education. A specialist in Russian-American relations, he also serves as the Director of the International Studies program.

ISBN 0-275-96099-4

EAN

9 780275 960995

90000>

HARDCOVER BAR CODE